HOW TO MAKE COFFEE

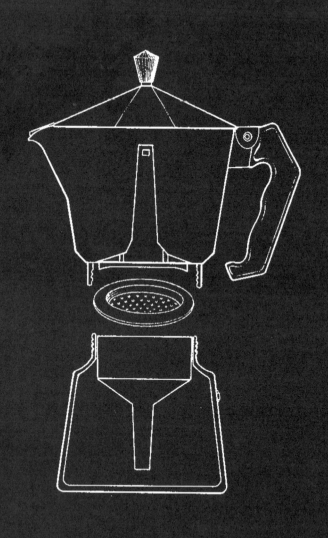

HOW TO MAKE COFFEE

THE SCIENCE BEHIND THE BEAN

LANI KINGSTON

IVY PRESS

This edition published in the UK in 2017 by
Ivy Press
An imprint of The Quarto Group
The Old Brewery, 6 Blundell Street
London N7 9BH, United Kingdom
T (0)20 7700 6700 **F** (0)20 7700 8066
www.QuartoKnows.com

First published in 2015

© 2017 Quarto Publishing plc

British Library Cataloguing-in-Publication Data
A catalogue record for this book is available
from the British Library

ISBN: 978-1-78240-518-4

This book was conceived, designed and
produced by
Ivy Press
58 West Street, Brighton BN1 2RA, UK

Creative Director: Peter Bridgewater
Publisher: Susan Kelly
Editorial Director: Tom Kitch
Art Director: James Lawrence
Commissioning Editor: Sophie Collins
Editor: Jo Richardson
Design & Graphics: Ginny Zeal
Illustrator: Sandra Pond

Printed in China

10 9 8 7 6 5 4 3 2 1

CONTENTS

INTRODUCTION

How to Make Coffee is not a recipe book, a bean anthology or a lifestyle accessory; it is an explanation of the scientific principles behind the art of coffee making, with clear step-by-step instructions explaining how all the major coffee-making methods work, and which beans, roast and grind are best for them.

Coffee percolated through to Europe around the time of the Renaissance. It came from Africa, where, according to one very appealing legend, it was discovered by goats – or at least by an observant goatherd who saw the effect a certain plant had on his livestock. It seems a very apposite product for its time: brought about by a blend of art, science, discovery and human curiosity, just the kind of refreshment needed by the Renaissance brain on full alert to process the breakthroughs, inventions, creativity and paradigm shifts of the era. Or maybe, given the effects of caffeine on the brain, it was one of the causes of the Renaissance . . .

Unlikely, but certainly it is the chemistry of coffee that makes it so compatible with the human body and brain, making it the world's favourite drink. The molecular structure of caffeine, the active ingredient, is very similar to a compound in the human body that controls part of the nervous system. This compound, adenosine, turns down nerve activity, while caffeine blocks adenosine from connecting with its receptors and as such can effectively re-energize.

Coffee is the result of trying to turn caffeine into something the human body can safely use. Growing, harvesting, processing, roasting, grinding, blending, mixing with water, applying heat, extracting, brewing, creating machinery to refine the processes: these are all science-driven applications. Understanding the science of coffee – its botany, geography, chemistry, physics, engineering – as well as the art – blending and balancing – helps to create the perfect cup of coffee. If you understand, for example, why water has to be a certain temperature, how the size of the coffee particles can affect extraction, what the ideal proportion of coffee solids to water is, the different rates at which compounds are soluble and how long brewing continues in the cup, you have grasped the principles behind coffee making, by whatever method, and you and your guest need never suffer a bitter cup of gritty, overboiled coffee or weak watery slop again.

The Bean

THE BEAN BELT

Coffee is one of the world's most valuable traded natural commodities, second only to oil, and it is produced and consumed worldwide. The prized bean is believed to have originally evolved in the wild in East Africa, but global exploration introduced it to many different cultures. Today, coffee is cultivated in more than seventy countries in an area known as 'the bean belt'.

THE BEGINNINGS OF COFFEE CULTURE

Although the precise origins of the consumption of coffee remain uncertain, it was likely first discovered in Ethiopia. It is thought that at some point before 1000 CE Ethiopian tribes began to grind the coffee fruits containing the coffee seeds or beans and mix them with an animal fat, making a kind of energy bar to sustain them on hunting trips or long journeys. Some nomadic tribes continue to consume these bars even today.

One popular legend has it that coffee's fortuitous introduction to the human race came about when a young Ethiopian goatherd found his goats prancing tirelessly after chewing on an unusual plant. Having sampled some of it himself and feeling energized as a consequence, the goatherd brought some of the magical plant back to his community. Word spread, and the rest is history.

The earliest evidence of human cultivation of the coffee plant has been traced back to the fifteenth century in Yemen. As with accounts of the discovery of coffee, just how it travelled to the Arabian Peninsula is largely a matter of conjecture. Some stories tell of Sudanese slaves chewing on coffee fruits to help them survive the journey from Ethiopia to Arabia; some tell of an Islamic scholar observing the invigorating effects of coffee on a trip to Ethiopia and bringing it back on his return to the Arabian Peninsula. Yet other tales view the spread of coffee simply as the result of the ongoing trade that existed between the two places.

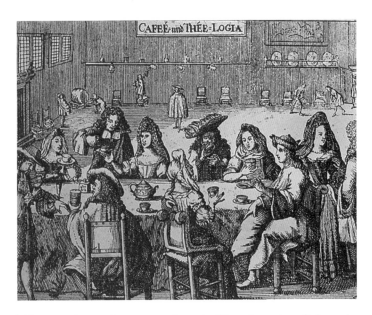

Whatever the precise course of events, fifteenth-century Sufi monks imbibed coffee as a beverage to help keep them awake during their nighttime prayers. It wasn't long before the drink became popular with the rest of the population, particularly the Muslims, who for religious reasons were barred from consuming intoxicating beverages, such as alcohol. Coffeehouses, known as *kaveh kanes*, multiplied throughout the Arab world, becoming communal hubs for socializing, education and general merriment.

Coffee became known as 'Arabian wine' or 'wine of Araby', and tales of this dark, bitter, stimulating beverage returned home with the thousands of pilgrims who visited Mecca every year. Venetian traders first introduced coffee to Europe in 1615, probably bringing the beans from the Middle East into Venice, where coffee soon became a fashionable beverage. By the 1650s, it was sold on the streets of Venice by lemonade vendors, along with liquor and chocolate, and the first European coffeehouse was opened there in the mid-1600s. Believed to have medicinal benefits, coffee was claimed to cure drunkenness, gout, smallpox and nausea, among other ailments.

HOW COFFEE WENT GLOBAL

While the drinking of coffee spread throughout the Middle East, westward into Europe and eastward into Persia and India in the sixteenth and early seventeenth centuries, and thereafter to the New World, the Arabs attempted to maintain a monopoly in the coffee trade by closely guarding its cultivation – they would boil or lightly roast coffee seeds before they were exported, to render them infertile. Despite their efforts, coffee cultivation began to extend beyond the Middle East in the seventeenth century, mainly due to the Dutch, who dominated international shipping trade at that time.

Attempts to cultivate coffee plants smuggled from Yemen to Europe in the early seventeenth century failed. However, when the Dutch took control of parts of Ceylon (now Sri Lanka) from the Portuguese in the mid-1600s, they found small coffee plantations begun with plants brought in by Arab traders, which they subsequently developed along with plantations established in their colonies on the Malabar Coast of India. In the late 1690s, they took coffee plants to their colony of Batavia (now Java), which became their main source of supply. From there, seeds were taken back to the *Hortus Botanicus* (botanical gardens) in Amsterdam and were successfully cultivated in greenhouses in 1706.

The first botanical description of the coffee tree, *Coffea arabica*, was made in these gardens by French botanist Antoine de Jussieu in 1713, and today coffee-loving pilgrims can come to the gardens to gaze on

Above left: An engraving of a seventeenth-century German coffeehouse.

TURKISH COFFEE BY LAW

Coffee was introduced to Turkey in the late fifteenth century and became an immensely popular beverage – so much so that Turkish law stated that a woman could divorce her husband if he did not provide her with a daily quota of coffee.

plants that have a direct lineage back to the eighteenth century. Their progenitors were to become the source of most of the cultivated coffee plants in the world today.

On a separate occasion, in 1670, the Sufi mystic Baba Budan reputedly smuggled seven coffee seeds from Yemen to the hills of Chikmagalur in Karnataka in southwest India, which was to become a renowned coffee-growing region.

Meanwhile, coffee's spread to the West is attributed to the Columbian Exchange: the transfer of plants, animals, ideas and diseases between the Eastern and Western hemispheres that followed Columbus' voyage to the New World of the Americas in 1492. Coffee and tea flowed one way, and chocolate in the other direction. The Dutch established coffee cultivation in their South American colony of Dutch Guiana (now Surinam) in the early eighteenth century, and at the same time, the mayor of Amsterdam presented the Sun King of France, Louis XIV, with a coffee plant from the *Hortus Botanicus*. A cutting from this plant was taken to the French Caribbean colony of Martinique by French naval officer Gabriel Mathieu de Clieu in 1723, and from there coffee spread to other Caribbean islands and to French Guiana. The story goes that coffee plants were smuggled into Brazil in 1727, leading to the beginnings of the world's largest coffee industry. With a happy circularity, Brazilian coffee plants were transported to Kenya and Tanganyika (now Tanzania) in East Africa in the late nineteenth century, bringing new coffee varietals to the area of the plant's wild origins in Ethiopia. Ethiopia has since become one of the top ten commercial coffee producers in the world.

In the New World, coffee became popular in Central and South America under the Spanish and Portuguese in the eighteenth century. In the British North American colonies, tea was the drink of choice until 1773, when the settlers rebelled against the heavy duty placed on it by the British government. Following the 1773 Boston Tea Party protest, coffee became the patriotic drink in the Thirteen Colonies that formed the United States following the War of Independence (1775–83).

Above: A shipment of tea is destroyed at the Boston Tea Party protest of 1773.

Today, the vast coffee-cultivation area known as 'the bean belt' sits almost entirely within the humid equatorial region between the two tropics, comprising growing regions that have steady temperatures of around 20°C (68°F), rich soil, moderate sunshine and rain. Many countries, economies and about twenty-five million people now depend upon coffee cultivation and export.

The world's top ten coffee-producing countries according to the International Coffee Organization (ICO) are Brazil, Vietnam, Colombia, Indonesia, Ethiopia, India, Mexico, Guatemala, Peru and Honduras. Brazil produces around one-third of the world's coffee. Some coffee connoisseurs say that Brazilian growers favour quantity over quality, but this misconception may relate back to a quota that was once placed on producers by the local coffee institute. Introduced in the early 1960s as part of the International Coffee Agreement, the quota system was designed to ensure equitable prices and a stable market. Various sources commented that high-quality beans may have been blended before export to meet weight quotas, resulting in an inferior product, because the different types of bean could not be evenly roasted together. Since the suspension of the quotas in the late 1980s, consumers have been increasingly able to purchase beans from a single estate, and the complexity, quality and variety of Brazilian beans is now evident. Because most farms in Brazil are small (70 per cent are smaller than 10 hectares/25 acres), the diversity and range of product is vast.

With all these countries producing coffee, as well as the various growing regions within the countries, the options to choose from when selecting coffee can be simply overwhelming, whether as a coffee buyer for a corporate coffeehouse or café or as a consumer. A coffee lover's only option is to taste, identify personal preferences and continue to be an analytical consumer. Various soils and terroirs can certainly produce beans with similarities if they are processed in the same way, so it is not just the growing location that dictates the flavour profile of a coffee bean. There are many different influencing factors at every step of the process, from climate conditions before the crop is harvested to the method used to extract that dark, aromatic liquid into your cup. This is why a Starbucks 'laboratory' in Amsterdam, for example, runs trials of new advances in coffee, creating and shaping trends that are then rolled out across the Continent. Their buyers taste beans from each estate every year, ordering the best selection from the crops available – while one year an Ethiopian Yirgacheffe might be of exceptional quality, next year the Sumatran Batak may rate more highly on the palates of the demanding coffee critics.

The home barista can become equally adept at coffee sampling with the many opportunities to continually explore the huge range available. That's the beauty of coffee – there are so many hundreds and thousands of combinations of beans, roasts, grinds and brewing methods that coffee lovers could spend a lifetime drinking a different cup every day.

THE BEAN BELT

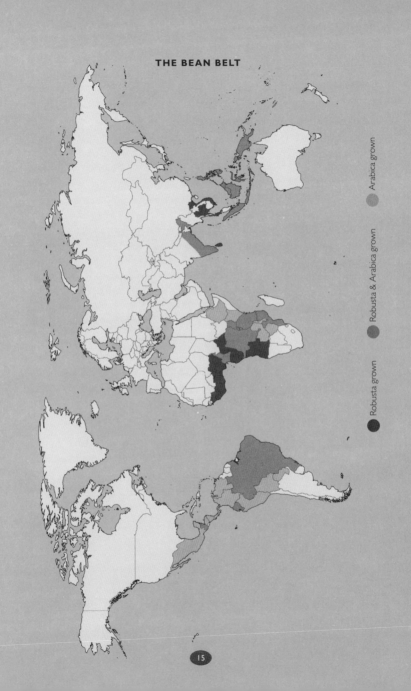

Robusta grown

Robusta & Arabica grown

Arabica grown

THE BEAN IDENTITY

There are more than five hundred genera in the Rubiaceae family, one of which is *Coffea*, with some six thousand species. Although botanists regard all seed-bearing plants that are part of the Rubiaceae family as coffee trees, the coffee trade is mainly concerned with just two species.

The coffee species of overwhelming importance are *Coffea arabica* and *C. canephora*; they make up the major percentage of coffee production. In general terms, coffee is divided into two main types, Arabica and Robusta, but botanically speaking, *C. arabica* has two main varities, Typica and Bourbon, and the most common form of *C. canephora* is the variety Robusta.

It is important to understand, however, that even within a single type of coffee, different and often unpredictable growing conditions and methods of processing will produce a varying flavour profile in the resulting cup of coffee, and a successful coffee bean may exhibit a completely distinct set of characteristics when grown in one location as compared to another. A prime example of this is Kona, the name reserved for Arabica beans grown only in the Kona district of Hawaii, because the specific environment gives the beans unique qualities that are not exhibited when grown elsewhere.

COFFEE FAMILY TREE

FAMILY	GENUS	SPECIES	VARIETY

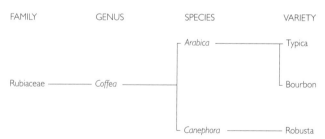

FAMILY: Rubiaceae — GENUS: *Coffea*

SPECIES: *Arabica* — VARIETY: Typica, Bourbon

SPECIES: *Canephora* — VARIETY: Robusta

ARABICA COFFEE

Despite containing less caffeine than Robusta coffee beans, Arabica coffee beans are considered superior in taste, smoother and less acidic. According to the ICO, more than 60 per cent of world coffee production comes from Arabica cultivars. This was the type of bean that started off the whole coffee story in Ethiopia, and it still grows best on high ground. The glorious-smelling flowers appear after a couple of years and produce ellipsoidal fruits, inside which are (usually two) flat seeds or coffee beans. The shrub can grow to 5 metres (15 ft), but to make it more commercially viable, it is usually pruned to about 2 metres (6 ft). Arabica has two sets of chromosomes, so it is capable of self-pollination, which means that its forms generally remain fairly stable because cross-pollination is less probable.

Of the two most common varieties of *Coffea arabica*, Typica was the first variety of the species to be discovered and, therefore, is regarded as the original coffee of the New World. It is a low-yielding variety that is valued for its excellent cup quality.

Bourbon varieties are often prized for their complex, balanced aromas and have spawned many high-quality mutations and subtypes, such as the natural mutations of Caturra, San Ramon and Pacas. There are also a number of Bourbon cultivars that have been propagated to suit the regional climate, environment and elevation – such as the prized Blue Mountain varieties, which only flourish at high altitudes. Other examples include Mundo Novo and Yellow Bourbon.

ARABICA

ROBUSTA COFFEE

Robusta is the most common 'varietal' of *Coffea canephora*, Arabica's more street-smart younger brother. Despite its flavour being considered less refined, Robusta is sometimes used in espresso blends, because it is known for producing a better crema – the creamy layer found on top of an espresso shot – than Arabica, and it is hardier

ROBUSTA

and more resistant to disease, especially coffee rust (*Hemileia vastatrix*). It also produces better yields and packs more caffeine. It is thought that the amplified caffeine content of Robusta, along with that of chlorogenic acids – naturally occurring antioxidants – is a result of the plant's self-protection mechanism in warding off pests and disease. When present at low levels, chlorogenic acids are considered an important part of a coffee's flavour profile. However, Robusta contains higher levels of these acids than other coffee species, and some studies show that oxidation products generated by these acids can introduce off-flavours, potentially compromising cup quality.[1]

Growing well at lower altitudes, Robusta thrives in areas where Arabica would be devastated by fungus and other diseases and pests. A stouter plant than Arabica and about twice the size, it grows well at higher humidity. After flowering, the berries take almost a year to ripen. The Robusta is self-sterile; therefore, cross-pollination by wind and bees and other insects is necessary for the plant to reproduce.

Although Robusta is a varietal and not a coffee species in itself – as in the case of Arabica – there are a number of subtypes of the Robusta bean, with each exhibiting a unique set of characteristics, such as greater immunity to disease and increased production capacity in comparison to Arabica.

[1] Farah, A., Monteiro, M., Calado, V., Franca, A., and Trugo, L. 2006. 'Correlation between cup quality and chemical attributes of Brazilian coffee.' *Food Chemistry*, 98, 373–380

LIBERICA COFFEE

Grown on a much smaller scale than *C. arabica* and *C. canephora*, the *C. liberica* plant is a much hardier species than either and is sometimes used as a replacement for plants of those species when they have experienced severe disease, such as coffee rust. Nevertheless, Liberica accounts for only 1 per cent of the world's coffee production because of low global demand due to the inferior quality of its beans. The leaves and fruits of the *C. liberica* plant are much larger than those of *C. arabica*, but the beans are distinctly bitter. They are sometimes used as a filler in blends with higher-quality beans.

WILD COFFEE & HYBRIDS

There are many other varieties of the coffee plant and some are used to make coffee; however, the produce may not be commonly traded, because it generally bears low economic value. Countless wild varieties, for example, can be found growing almost exclusively in their natural environments. Because these habitats are being destroyed by human intervention, conscious efforts to collect samples of each of these species are taking place around the globe in an attempt to preserve biodiversity. As part of its biodiversity programme, World Coffee Research (WCR) is collecting and preserving wild Arabica coffee samples from Ethiopia and South Sudan. The genetic base of cultivated forms of Arabica is severely restricted, so cataloguing the wild varities will help ensure that genetic variety can be exploited in future breeding programmes.

Since the Green Revolution of the 1960s and 1970s, when scientists began developing high-yielding crops and started to use agrochemicals on a global basis, hybridized coffee plants have become increasingly propagated on farms and plantations worldwide. Although scientifically genetically modified (GM) coffee has not (and probably will not) become commercialized, scientists have long been modifying varieties 'naturally' by crossbreeding and other methods. Modern varieties of coffee that are drought-, pest- and disease-resistant, heavier bearing and faster to reach maturity are replacing many original varieties that were once commonly grown. For example, Ruiru Eleven is resistant to coffee berry disease and coffee leaf rust, is high yielding, and can be planted at twice the normal density.

There are many ways in which the Green Revolution has benefited farmers (larger crops, easier harvesting, guaranteed income), but one of its major downsides, it has been argued, is that the reduction in biodiversity not only leaves crops open to devastation in the case of a new disease, but these new crops also often require human intervention to survive. If a farmer cannot afford agrochemicals, for example, his plantation could fail.

While this may cast a gloom over the future of coffee agriculture, what it really comes down to here and now is how these varieties perform during the transition from the plantation to your cup. Many coffee aficionados largely condemn hybrid varieties, characterizing them as lacking in complexity of flavour. Some varieties, however, have been specifically combined for their taste, aroma and flavour profiles, bringing together and complementing the best qualities of each original bean, rather than being developed solely to make them easier or more profitable for the farmer to grow. Other coffee varieties are natural hybrids created by two compatible species crossbreeding without human involvement. Regardless, hybrid coffees can still create a great cup in the same way any other variety of coffee can, as long as the bean itself is up to the task.

In summary, the only true way to select a bean is to be an informed, analytical consumer. While it is important to know your Arabica from your Robusta, and your Typica from your Bourbon, it is not as simple as selecting any old Arabica bean and expecting it to deliver a high-quality brew. Peer review, speaking with local baristas and roasters and, most important, tasting and trying as many varieties as you can from the colossal range offered are the only ways to be sure that you are selecting the best beans available from this year's crop – and the beans most suited to your own personal preferences.

THE ANATOMY OF COFFEE

Let us go back to coffee's roots and look at the plant itself. Long before they are transformed into the dark brown coffee beans we are familiar with, these coffee seeds can be found at the heart of the fruits growing in bunches along the branches of the coffee tree.

The coffee tree has evergreen leaves that are shiny on the upper side, and produces clusters of white, fragrant flowers along the branches of the tree that form into fruits. These fruits are drupes, classified as such by the fact that they do not split at maturity, and they are made up of a soft, fleshy exterior with a shell inside that hosts the seed that we know as the coffee bean. Coffee fruits, which are more commonly called berries or cherries in the coffee industry, develop a diameter of about 1.5 centimetres (⅝ in) and are made up of two distinct parts: the **outer pericarp**, which encases the **seeds** within.

The pericarp is comprised of three layers. The skin, known as the **epicarp**, is the outermost layer, initially green but ripening to a brilliant shade of red or yellow. The second layer consists of the flesh of the fruit, the **mesocarp**, more commonly known as mucilage. Exceptionally sweet, how this layer of fruit is treated during processing is instrumental in determining the flavour of the end product – methods that retain the mucilage for as long as possible during processing generally lead to a berrylike sweetness, absorbed from the fermentation of the mucilage. The final layer is the **endocarp**, usually referred to as the parchment or hull, which is the shell that encases the coffee seed.

Underneath this parchment layer lies the coffee seed, which also consists of three layers: the outer **spermoderm**, commonly known as silver skin; the **endosperm**, the most important part of the coffee bean in defining its eventual flavour and aroma profile; and the inner **embryo**, the heart of the coffee bean itself.

The spermoderm is a thin coating that wraps around the seed. It is generally removed before roasting, but some traces often remain, flaking off during the roasting process. The endosperm, a source of carbohydrates, provides the growing seedling with nutrients. Rich in polysaccharides, the cells of the endosperm also contain proteins and minerals. Among the many elements that contribute to the particular flavour and aroma characteristics of the coffee bean that reside here are chlorogenic acids, lipids and caffeine.

The inner embryo occupies a small amount of space, because most of the seed is taken up by its food supply, but this tiny integral part is what develops into a new plant when supplied with moisture and food.

Within each fruit there are usually two seeds; less than 10 per cent of the world's coffee fruits produce only one. Botanists have observed that these single-seed fruits, known as peaberries, occur when only one of the ovaries is pollinated. Fans of the peaberry claim that they are sweeter, richer and more flavoursome, because, they argue, the nutrients and compounds normally split between two seeds are concentrated into one. However, others regard peaberries as a detrimental genetic mutation and believe that a high incidence of peaberries is a sign of plant infertility.

COFFEE FRUIT

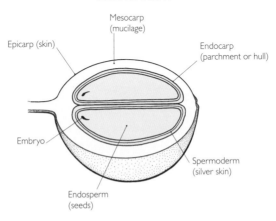

Mesocarp (mucilage)

Epicarp (skin)

Endocarp (parchment or hull)

Embryo

Spermoderm (silver skin)

Endosperm (seeds)

HIGH OR LOW?

Although numerous factors contribute in varying degrees to determining a coffee bean's flavour, as with wine, the terroir – the geography, geology and climate of its growing place – has an undeniably profound effect on its taste profile.

High altitudes are considered ideal for growing the coffee plant, with cooler temperatures delaying the growth cycle, which allows the bean to go through a longer maturation process, thus creating a much fuller, richer and more pronounced flavour. This extended maturation process also ensures that the beans are imbued with the flavours typical of the region in which they are grown. High-elevation beans retain their flavour longer in storage because their extended development produces a harder bean. Scientific studies comparing high- and low-altitude beans have determined that high-altitude beans have a far superior body and aroma.[2] *Coffea arabica* grows best at high altitudes, though it is more expensive to grow – not only does it have a longer maturation period but it is also generally selectively picked instead of being strip-picked (see pages 25–26), resulting in a relatively low yield.

Low-altitude coffee plants produce higher yields due to faster ripening times, but the beans need to be treated differently than those from higher altitudes – all the way from roast to brew. With low-elevation varieties producing a much softer bean due to their fast development, they are not as tolerant of darker roasts. Best when lightly roasted, the flavour profile is often described as 'earthy, muddy, simple or bland'. Robusta coffee grows well at lower altitudes because it is better suited to tougher conditions, such as higher temperatures and consequent potential fungal contamination.

The diagram on page 24 attempts to classify the flavour profiles characteristic of coffee beans grown at different altitudes, high through

[2] Avelino, J., Barboza, B., Araya, J. C., Fonseca, C., Davrieux, F., Guyot, B., and Cilas, C. 2005. 'Effects of slope exposure, altitude, and yield on coffee quality in two altitude terroirs of Costa Rica, Orosi, and Santa María de Dota.' *Journal of the Science of Food and Agriculture* 85 (11): 1869–76

low, though these can only serve as a guide due to the many other influencing factors involved in coffee cultivation and production. However, generally speaking, the longer maturation process of higher-altitude beans leads to complex sugar formation, which yields deeper flavour, whereas lower-altitude beans are generally milder and less acidic.

Additionally, the altitude at which the coffee plant is grown is a major factor in the chemical make-up of the bean. Robusta has a much higher caffeine content than Arabica, and this is said to offer the plant natural insecticidal properties, adding to the sturdy nature of the variety and helping make it better able to withstand the environmental stresses present at low altitudes. Some scientists believe that Arabica has evolved to contain lower levels of caffeine because its bitterness as a defense against insects is not an imperative on higher ground.

FLAVOUR PROFILES

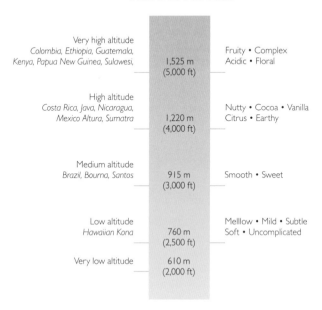

Very high altitude
Colombia, Ethiopia, Guatemala, Kenya, Papua New Guinea, Sulawesi,
1,525 m (5,000 ft)
Fruity • Complex Acidic • Floral

High altitude
Costa Rica, Java, Nicaragua, Mexico Altura, Sumatra
1,220 m (4,000 ft)
Nutty • Cocoa • Vanilla Citrus • Earthy

Medium altitude
Brazil, Bourna, Santos
915 m (3,000 ft)
Smooth • Sweet

Low altitude
Hawaiian Kona
760 m (2,500 ft)
Melllow • Mild • Subtle Soft • Uncomplicated

Very low altitude
610 m (2,000 ft)

BRINGING IN THE BEANS

There are two methods of harvesting the fruits of the coffee tree: strip picking, where the entire crop is harvested through one pass of the plantation, or selective picking, the harvesting by hand of only the bright red, fully ripe berries.

STRIP PICKING

This method of harvesting is carried out either mechanically or by hand, but in both cases the coffee plants are stripped of all fruits in one go. With mechanical strip picking, harvesting machines run along the fields, knocking the fruit down with revolving arms. Gatherers follow, picking up the fruits from tarpaulins that cover the ground and placing them in baskets or bags while separating the berries from twigs and other natural debris. Otherwise, workers simply run their hands down the branches, brushing all the fruits onto the tarpaulin or into a bag placed under the branch being harvested. Back in the processing plant, the fruits run through a sorting machine, picking out the ripe, sound ones from the overripe and underripe, damaged or rotting.

A strip picker can gather up to 250 kilograms (550 lb) of fruit per day, but with this method, substandard fruit can easily pass through the sorting process, thereby reducing the quality of the final crop.

SELECTIVE PICKING

This method of harvesting generally produces a finer-quality coffee bean because each fruit is selected at its optimum ripeness, but because it is labour-intensive, it is generally reserved for Arabica beans. Workers hand-select only the perfect fruits and carefully place them in their baskets. Each and every tree will be revisited many times throughout the season until all the fruit has been picked at its peak.

Workers quickly analyse the fruit to determine its ripeness, using a number of indicators, such as colour and firmness. Perfectly ripe fruits should be relatively soft and the seed able to be squeezed out by hand.

If the fruit is too hard, it is underripe, but if too soft, it is overripe and much of the pulp and mucilage will have broken down. This reduction of the pericarp layers can lead to damage to the bean during pulping, because there is not enough mucilage present for the fruit to slide through the pulper with ease. A similar problem occurs with underripe fruits, where mucilage has not yet developed to a sufficient degree. With selective picking, a worker can usually harvest about 100 kilograms (220 lb) of fruit per day.

The type of harvesting methods used around the world depend upon the crop's ripening time and the specific growing environment. In Brazil, for example, the uniform temperature and flat landscape mean that the whole crop can be strip-picked when 75 per cent or more of the crop is ready. In this scenario, separating and discarding the overripe or underripe berries is more cost-effective than hand-selecting only the ripe berries and then allowing the rest to remain on the plant to ripen.

After planting, coffee trees often take three to five years to bear fruit, depending on the variety. Each tree yields 2 to 4 kilograms (4½ to 9 lb) of fruit per season, although yields vary annually and are dependent upon environmental factors, the age of the tree and the soil.

Processing the fruits should begin as soon as possible after harvest. Various recommendations advise that the process should be started no later than twenty-four hours after picking the fruit,[3] but many plantations will not leave the fruit for longer than ten hours before processing. The fruit sugars start to convert to starches as soon as the fruits leave the tree, and deteriorating fruits will rapidly reduce the quality of the crop. The mucilage layer breaks down quickly, reducing the protective layer surrounding the coffee beans. This can lead to damage to the beans during pulping in the same way as do overripe and underripe fruits. The fruit also begins to lose moisture immediately following harvest. Crops are often sold by weight and, therefore, the longer the fruit is left before processing, the lower the crop's value.

[3] Queensland Government. October 23, 2013. 'Coffee Processing at Home.' Accessed June 22, 2014. http://www.daff.qld.gov.au/plants/fruit-and-vegetables/specialty-crops/coffee-processing-in-the-home

PROCESSING THE CROP

After harvesting, the coffee fruits are processed to remove the layers of mucilage and pulp from the green seeds and the seeds are dried to a specific moisture content – the first stage in turning them into a product suitable for grinding and extraction into a beverage.

There are two primary methods of processing the coffee fruits – the dry and wet methods – but increasing in popularity is a third, recently developed 'semi-washed' method. The term encompasses varying processing techniques depending on the country of production.

THE DRY METHOD

Also known as the natural method, this way of processing coffee beans is frequently used in countries with limited access to water. This method requires little machinery and is the oldest, most traditional way of processing coffee. It involves leaving the fruits intact and laying them out to dry whole.

First, the coffee fruits are cleaned either by pressurized air or water. The use of water at this stage has the added benefit of sorting the fruits at the same time, because the unripe ones float to the top and can be easily skimmed from the batch.

The fruits are subsequently laid out on mats, in vats or on concrete slabs and raked throughout the day and then covered at night for protection. This procedure is often continued for several weeks until the moisture content is reduced to 10 to 12 per cent. This stage of the processing is one of the most important, because overdrying can produce brittle beans, and layering the fruit too thickly can result in fungal and bacterial contamination.

Most Robusta coffee is processed using this traditional dry method, as is the majority of Arabica grown in Brazil. It is often thought to produce an inferior bean, because the potential for inconsistency,

DRY METHOD

Coffee Beans

| Air or water cleaning |

↓

| Baking and drying |

↓

| Hulling |

WET METHOD

Coffee Beans

| Washing |

↓

| Flotation separation |

↓

| Pulping |

↓

| Fermentation |

↓

| Rinsing |

↓

| Drying |

damage or contamination is higher than with other methods. However, this method tends to produce a more complex bean that is heavier in body, and because the fruit is left on the bean longer, the flavour of the coffee is more pronounced and the sweetness of the fruit transfers to the green seed. Naturally processed coffees are known for their rich body and sweet, wild berry flavours.

Once the fruits have been dried, they can be stored in silos while waiting for other stages of processing. After this maturation period, they are transported to factories to be processed by large milling machines that separate out the prized centres from the shrivelled fruits. This process is known as hulling. The extracted beans are then sorted and those with defects discarded, while the remaining are graded and packaged for shipping to roasters around the world.

THE WET METHOD

This method of processing coffee, also known as the washed method, is usually employed in only wealthier coffee-growing areas, because it requires a large quantity of water and a range of expensive machinery. Being a largely machine-driven process, it is known for producing a better-quality coffee, because the potential for defective beans making their way into the final batch through human error is reduced.

Poured into water tanks, the fruits are first washed and then transported down water channels. Flotation separation occurs, with screens sorting fruits according to size and ripeness. Pulp is removed from the fruits as they pass between a fixed and a moving surface, with the machine removing the skin and flesh to leave only the seeds and mucilage. Continuing on to fermentation tanks, the seeds are left to ferment for between twelve and eighty hours, depending on the different characteristics of each crop. While in these tanks, enzymes present in the coffee fruits break down the mucilage. Sometimes water is added, but generally the moisture from the mucilage itself will create an environment that is perfect for fermentation. A simple touch test can determine whether the mucilage has been broken down enough

– seeds rubbed between the hands should have a gritty texture. In some cases, the mucilage is removed mechanically instead of through fermentation. There are coffee experts who advocate the traditional fermentation process, but cupping tests (see page 44) have shown that there is often little difference between the two methods.

The coffee seed, left inside its parchment coating, is rinsed to remove any remaining mucilage, and then the drying process starts. The beans are laid out in the sun on patios or drying beds, as in the traditional method, or are dried in mechanical driers – or using a combination of the two – until the moisture content has been reduced to the requisite 10 to 12 per cent. At this point, the coffee is referred to as parchment coffee due to the yellow parchment layer attached to the seed.

One last stage of hulling takes place to remove the parchment and reveal the green coffee beans underneath, and then they are ready to be shipped to coffee roasters, extractors and soluble coffee producers.

At least 50 per cent of the world's coffee is processed using the wet method, because it delivers greater batch consistency and a cleaner, crisper coffee. Consistency is important in maintaining international trade partnerships, and because coffee is one of the largest export commodities on the planet, these partnerships are sought after and highly valued. The wet method reduces spoilage and quality reduction due to human error or environmental conditions, because each stage of the process can be controlled. While dry processing is less costly, the wet method (and the introduction of mechanical processes) can increase yield, reduce labour and ensure a consistency of flavour.

SEMI-WASHED METHODS

A more recent way of processing coffee is the semi-washed, or pulped natural method, which in some ways is a combination of the major dry and wet methods. Mainly used for speciality coffee production, it has developed as a consequence of the experimentation that the popularity and global demand for coffee has sparked.

The semi-washed method follows the same process as the washed method up until the fruit is pulped, and then the beans are dried with the mucilage still attached, skipping the fermentation stage. Because the sticky layer of mucilage prevents the drying of the seeds mechanically, sun-drying is a necessity, resulting in characteristics similar to those produced through the traditional method, such as sweetness and reduced acidity.

All coffees that retain this layer of mucilage during the drying process are referred to as semi-washed, but the method of processing nevertheless differs among coffee-producing countries, which has led to some confusion in the industry as to exactly what the term means. Indonesian wet hulling, for example, is also often categorized as semi-washed, although it is actually a different process than the pulped natural method used in Central America. Wet hulling involves a short fermentation that does not remove all of the mucilage, an initial drying to achieve 40 per cent moisture content before hulling, and then a subsequent resumption of the drying process to achieve the final 10 to 12 per cent moisture level.

In Costa Rica, semi-washed coffee is also known as *miel*, or 'honeyed coffee', because the fruit brings a degree of sweetness to the bean. The process used in this case entails drying the beans to the full 10 to 12 per cent moisture content with the mucilage still attached.

There are a number of seemingly minor elements of coffee processing that can result in major changes to the end product. For instance, coffee beans that are quickly dried in stable environmental conditions generally have a cleaner, crisper flavour than those that are dried slowly, which taste fruitier.

The processing method is perhaps one of the most important influencing factors in the eventual flavour profile of the coffee bean that ends up in your cup. Whether you are seeking sweetness, fruitiness or acidity, being aware of how a coffee bean has been processed can help inform your bean selection.

The Chemistry

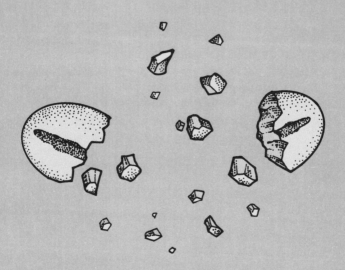

MOLECULAR COMPATIBILITY

One of the many reasons we like coffee so much is that there is sympathy between human and coffee biochemistry at a molecular level. Many of the energizing effects of the caffeine contained in coffee are due to its interaction with the adenosine receptors in the brain, which play an important role in energy transfer.

When you are awake, the neurons in your brain are continually firing, and a by-product of this firing is adenosine, a biochemical compound that is a neuromodulator for the central nervous system. Your nervous system receptors are constantly monitoring your levels of adenosine, and when they get too high, your brain will slow down neural activity and dilate the blood vessels, making you feel sleepy or crave rest.

Caffeine has a similar molecular structure to adenosine – notably, two nitrogen rings. This similarity in structure means that caffeine can bind to your nervous system's adenosine receptors without activating them, effectively blocking the receptors from detecting the levels of adenosine and, therefore, keeping you alert even if those levels may be elevated.

MOLECULAR STRUCTURES

CAFFEINE
$C_8H_{10}N_4O_2$

ADENOSINE
$C_{10}H_{16}N_5O_{13}P_3$

THE CAFFEINE HIT

Pure caffeine is a white, bitter and odourless powder, an organic chemical that belongs to a class of chemicals called purine alkaloids. It occurs in several plant species that are used to make beverages (including cocoa, tea, yerba mate and guarana). It acts as a pesticide against some insects but sharpens the memories of others, which helps increase the return rate of insect pollinators.

One study showed that honeybees were three times more likely to remember a floral scent after ingesting caffeine, helping to ensure their return and, in turn, the reproductive success of the plant.[1] In humans, it has mild diuretic properties and acts as a mild stimulant on the nervous, circulatory and respiratory systems.

Once consumed, caffeine is absorbed through the gastrointestinal tract and can remain in your system for between four and six hours. When it reaches the liver, it is metabolized into three compounds. Most of it turns into **paraxanthine**, which increases the breakdown of lipids in the bloodstream; a small amount becomes **theobromine**, which dilates blood vessels and increases the production of urine; and a tiny amount becomes **theophylline**, which relaxes smooth muscle (the kind found in the digestive tract and respiratory system). The result is that the heart rate quickens, the muscles receive more blood but the skin and organs receive less and the liver releases glycogen. Because it is both fat- and water-soluble, caffeine passes easily through the blood–brain barrier.

Caffeine encourages the production of epinephrine (adrenaline) and increases the levels of neurotransmitters, such as dopamine, serotonin and acetylcholine, all of which are responsible for mood changes, among other things. Working in a similar way to adrenaline, caffeine increases breathing as well as the heart rate, resulting in a short burst of energy. Perhaps one of the primary reasons for coffee's popularity is its ability to increase mental alertness with practically no negative side effects.

[1] Wright, G., Baker, D., Palmer, M., Stabler, D., Mustard, J., Power, E., et al. 2013. 'Caffeine in Floral Nectar Enhances a Pollinator's Memory of Reward.' *Science* 339 (6124): 1202–1204

Caffeine has been tested for numerous health benefits. It has been linked to increased metabolism and muscle strength as well as decreased risk of diabetes, cancer and heart disease, along with many other positive effects. Because it is a widely consumed stimulant, it is fortunate that studies show that it is non-addictive due to the fact that it does not activate reward circuits in the brain.[2]

However, while caffeine is not addictive, those who consume more than four to five cups of coffee a day can develop a mild physical dependence. This can be accompanied by withdrawal symptoms when coffee consumption is stopped suddenly, such as headaches, fatigue, irritability or anxiety, but symptoms usually abate within a few days. If coffee consumption is reduced gradually instead of halted abruptly, these withdrawal effects can be mostly avoided.

CAFFEINE METABOLITES

CAFFEINE

PARAXANTHINE   THEOBROMINE   THEOPHYLLINE

[2] Boyet, S., and Nehlig, A. 2000. 'Dose-response study of caffeine effects on cerebral functional activity with a specific focus on dependence.' *Brain Research* 858 (1): 71–77

WHAT'S IN YOUR CUP?

The chemical components of green coffee and roasted coffee differ substantially, because fundamental changes take place within the bean during processing and roasting. The chemical make-up of coffee beans also varies according to species, geographical location, soil condition, climate and other environmental factors.

Nevertheless, the basic constituents of the coffee bean, whether roasted or unroasted, remain largely the same – the main difference lies in the proportions in which they are present. A coffee bean consists of water, amino acids, sugars, carbohydrates, fibre, proteins, organic acids (such as chlorogenic acids), minerals, lipids, caffeine and trigonelline, an alkaloid responsible for the bitterness of a brew. More than eight hundred chemicals have been indentified in coffee beans, many of them providing flavours, aromas and/or health benefits.

PHENOLS & ANTIOXIDANTS

Caffeine is the most well-known chemical present in coffee beans; however, the beans contain many others that are equally important, such as phenolic acids, which have high antioxidant activity. These antioxidants are among the richest sources of polyphenols in the Western diet, similar to those found in berries, and they also contain potent flavonoids and lignans.

The most prevalent phenols in green coffee are chlorogenic acids, which account for much of its antioxidant content. A large proportion of coffee's chlorogenic acids are destroyed during the roasting process, with only 20 per cent remaining. However, tests have shown that roasted coffee beans have a higher antioxidant component than their unroasted counterparts.[3] So how can this be the case when the most powerful antioxidant source present in the green bean is largely lost through roasting?

[3] Šlebodova, A., Brezova, V., and Staško, A. 2009. 'Coffee as a source of antioxidants: An EPR study.' *Food Chemistry*, 114, 859–868

Roasting causes the coffee bean to undergo a series of structural changes, leading to the synthesizing of various compounds and melanoidins, which are potent antioxidants. Melanoidins are of great interest to scientists because they have strong antioxidant, antifungal, antimicrobial, anti-inflammatory and antihypertensive properties. The synthesizing of various antioxidants during roasting has been attributed in part to the Maillard reaction – a chemical reaction between sugars and amino acids, resulting in the familiar browning that occurs in many foods during cooking. One of the most important processes in cooking, the reaction creates many new flavour compounds, contributing significantly to the final flavour profile.

Tests show that the green Robusta bean has a higher antioxidant content than the Arabica.[4] However, these antioxidants are highly susceptible to damage and destruction during roasting, leaving Arabica once again on top with a higher antioxidant content in the final, completely processed product. Other factors also affect the antioxidant content, with studies showing that geographical area, type of bean and terroir all play a part in determining the amount present. For example, Arabica coffee fruits from plants grown in Mexico and India have been found to contain higher levels of chlorogenic acids compared to those harvested from equivalent plants cultivated in China.

It has been well established that polyphenols and phenols can increase plasma antioxidant capacity, which can help protect human cells against oxidative damage, thus reducing the risk of various associated degenerative diseases.

[4] Richelle, M., Tavazzi, I., and Offord, E. 2001. 'Comparison of the Antioxidant Activity of Commonly Consumed Polyphenolic Beverages (Coffee, Cocoa, and Tea) Prepared per Cup Serving.' *Journal of Agricultural and Food Chemistry* 49 (7): 3438–3442

ROASTED ARABICA

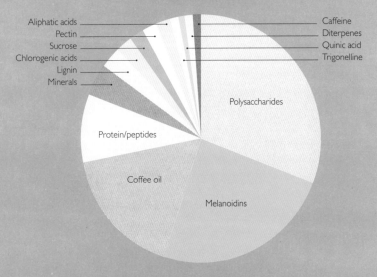

Aliphatic acids
Pectin
Sucrose
Chlorogenic acids
Lignin
Minerals

Caffeine
Diterpenes
Quinic acid
Trigonelline

Polysaccharides

Protein/peptides

Coffee oil

Melanoidins

GREEN ARABICA

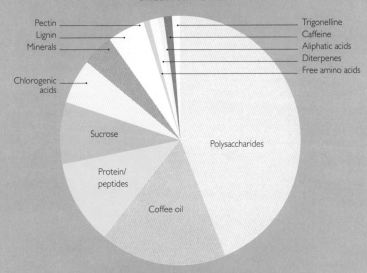

Pectin
Lignin
Minerals

Chlorogenic acids

Sucrose

Protein/peptides

Coffee oil

Trigonelline
Caffeine
Aliphatic acids
Diterpenes
Free amino acids

Polysaccharides

Graphic adapted from figures in *Coffee: Emerging Health Effects and Disease Prevention* (2012, Oxford, John Wiley & Sons)

ROASTED ROBUSTA

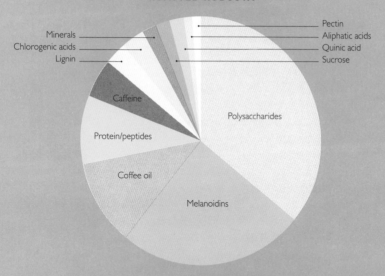

Minerals
Chlorogenic acids
Lignin

Pectin
Aliphatic acids
Quinic acid
Sucrose

Caffeine

Protein/peptides

Coffee oil

Melanoidins

Polysaccharides

GREEN ROBUSTA

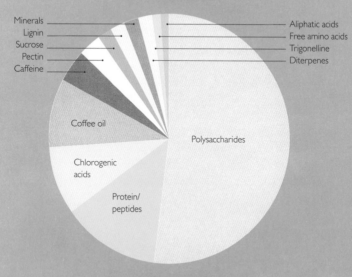

Minerals
Lignin
Sucrose
Pectin
Caffeine

Aliphatic acids
Free amino acids
Trigonelline
Diterpenes

Coffee oil

Chlorogenic acids

Protein/peptides

Polysaccharides

LIPIDS

Lipids, which are organic compounds such as fats and oils, play an important role in the quality of your cup of coffee. Primarily composed of triacylglycerols, sterols and tocopherols (vitamin E), these lipids all contribute unique qualities. Diterpenes are fatty acids that can comprise up to 20 per cent of the lipid content, and they are difficult to classify, because studies have shown both positive and negative effects on health resulting from their consumption. Cafestol and kahweol, two diterpenes present in the largest quantities in unfiltered brews, have been proven to raise serum cholesterol in humans.[5] Paper filters successfully trap most of these compounds, so arguably those at risk of cardiovascular disease should either drink unfiltered coffee in moderation or stick to filtered methods. Conversely, however, some studies show that cafestol and kahweol can reduce the effect of certain carcinogens.[6]

Most of these fatty acid compounds may decompose if coffee is stored above ideal temperatures, lending off-flavours to the coffee, but lipids remain largely intact during roasting because of their high melting points. However, the type of brewing method used can reduce the lipid content to a varying degree, with filtration depleting it by a significant amount. Studies have shown that filter brewing methods retain only 7 milligrams of lipids, while boiling and espresso processes retain anywhere between 60 to 160 milligrams per 150-millilitre (5-oz) cup.[7] A large proportion of coffee flavours are contained within these fatty acid compounds, explaining why filtered coffee has a different mouthfeel when compared to coffee brewed by non-filtered methods. With almost double the lipid content of the Robusta bean, it is no wonder that the Arabica variety is known for its superior cup quality.

[5] Urgert, R., Essed, N., van der Weg, G., Kosmeijer-Schuil, T., and Katan, M. 1997. 'Separate effects of the coffee diterpenes cafestol and kahweol on serum lipids and liver aminotransferases.' *The American Journal of Clinical Nutrition* 65 (2): 519–524

[6] Calvin, C., Holzhaeuser, D., Scharf, G., Constable, A., Huber, W., and Schilter, B. 2002. 'Cafestol and kahweol, two coffee-specific diterpenes with anticarcinogenic activity.' *Food and Chemical Toxicology* 40 (8): 1155–1163

[7] Ratnayake, W., Hollywood, R., O'Grady, E., and Stavric, B. (1993). 'Lipid content and composition of coffee brews prepared by different methods.' *Food and Chemical Toxicology* 13 (4): 263–269

ACIDS

There are more than thirty separate organic acids found in the roasted coffee bean, and each contributes something different to the flavour or antioxidant content. Chlorogenic acids are perhaps the most important, making up a large proportion of the acid content and providing much of the antioxidant content in your cup. When the beans are roasted, around half the chlorogenic acids are destroyed in the production of quinic acid and caffeic acid. Quinic acid is important for cup quality and flavour, forming coloured compounds during the Maillard reaction (see page 42) and producing melanoidins, a potent antioxidant. Quinic acid also contributes to perceived bitterness and astringency, and caffeic acid is an active antioxidant that is also present in wine.

In terms of flavour, acidity is a major defining factor. The balance of acids in your cup determines how your coffee will taste and, if correctly balanced, will prevent it from tasting flat (see page 43).

ALKALOIDS

Trigonelline is a bitter alkaloid present in both the green and roasted coffee bean, and while it certainly contributes significantly to the aromas, flavours and cup profile (see page 43), it is also the source of a number of health benefits. During roasting, trigonelline deteriorates and produces a number of compounds, including nicotinic acid, better known as vitamin B_3 or niacin. A single cup of coffee can contain anywhere between 1 and 3 milligrams. The U.S. National Institute of Health (NIH) recommends an overall daily intake of 12 to 16 milligrams of niacin per day, depending upon gender and age.

MINERALS

Coffee contains potassium, phosphorus, magnesium, manganese and trace amounts of about thirty other minerals. However, it should not be relied upon as a significant source of minerals, because the content varies widely according to the type of bean and its growing conditions.

FLAVOUR, TASTE & AROMA

Around a thousand chemical compounds have been identified within the humble coffee bean, although the exact number is revised on an almost annual basis. The beans are unassuming to look at, but their chemical make-up is surprisingly complex.

The chemical composition of the coffee end product largely depends on the roasting style used. The roasting process turns carbohydrates and fats into aromatic oils and breaks down or builds up various acids. These and many more chemical reactions determine the final aroma, flavour and taste of your cup. During roasting, two major processes take place, forming the majority of the flavour and aroma compounds that are present in coffee.

THE MAILLARD REACTION

As previously mentioned, the Maillard reaction takes place during baking, roasting and other cooking processes, and it involves the rearranging or degrading of amino acids and simple sugars in a molecular reaction that enhances, adds and determines flavour.

THE STRECKER DEGRADATION

The Strecker degradation is a chemical reaction that also involves amino acids, but in this case combined with carbonyl compounds, resulting in the important flavour compounds ketones and aldehydes. As in the Maillard reaction, these are produced mainly during the roasting process.

Many of the chemicals contained within the coffee bean contribute in some way to the flavour profile, but certain groups of chemicals are known to provide the majority of flavours and aromas, as detailed on the following pages.

ACIDITY

While acidity in many food items is often tied to sour flavours, acidity in coffee relates to the many levels of nuanced flavours that give the cup dimension. Varying levels of different acids lend different individual flavours and, if these are well balanced, they provide complex, snappy composite flavours that give coffee its zing. The greatest proportion of coffee's acid content is made up of chlorogenic acids (see page 41), and second in line are citric acids, adding brightness to a cup in small to moderate quantities but less desirable sour notes in higher quantities. Also important are malic, acetic and phosphoric acids. Malic acids lend fruity apple notes, acetic acid gives the brew a distinctly winelike flavour and phosphoric acid adds no flavour but a sparkling, biting acidity.

KETONES & ALDEHYDES

Formed during the roasting process by the interaction of oxygen and carbohydrates, ketones are responsible for 21.5 per cent of coffee aroma and aldehydes 50.7 per cent, according to mass spectral analysis of coffee grounds.[8]

There are dozens of different types of ketones and aldehydes present in both green and roasted coffee, each providing distinct and unique flavours and aromas that vary considerably – some are floral, sweet, fruity or honeylike, but others can be bitter, nutty or burning. Similarly, various ketones are described as anything from buttery, spicy and herbaceous to fruity or minty. The ketone and aldehyde aromas are the most delicate but also some of the most volatile.

TRIGONELLINE

As we have seen, the alkaloid trigonelline in coffee beans breaks down during roasting to produce vitamins that are essential to human health (see page 41) but also volatile aromatic compounds, such as pyrrols,

[8] Merritt, C., Bazinet, M., Sullivan, J., and Robertson, D. 1963. 'Mass Spectrometric Determination of the Volatile Components from Ground Coffee.' *Journal of Agricultural and Food Chemistry* 11: 152–155

pyridines and pyrazines. These compounds provide a substantial amount of the aroma in coffee, and, as such, trigonelline directly contributes to the profile of your cup. A bitter compound, trigonelline is significantly reduced the longer coffee beans are roasted. Pyrrols often impart undesirable flavours, such as earthy, musty, mushroom or caramel-like aromas; pyridines are often harsh, contributing nutty, burnt or astringent aromas but sometimes floral notes; and pyrazines, as the second most prevalent class of aromatic compounds in coffee, deliver flavours of toast, nuts or grain.

SUCROSE

Sucrose is the most common sugar in coffee, but it is largely destroyed during roasting. Carbohydrates such as sucrose are imperative for the Maillard reaction (see page 42) and form the basis of caramelization – the process of browning the sugars – which is one of the major sources of flavour and aroma in coffee. Furans are a result of the pyrolysis (the decomposition of organic compounds when subjected to extreme heat) of sugars, such as sucrose and polysaccharides, and are sweet, nutty, caramel-like or roasty. Caramelization retains the sweetness but adds flavour and aroma as well as a slight bitterness through the loss of water from the sugar molecule.

THE CUPPING METHOD OF ASSESSMENT

Having identified the key elements that make up coffee's flavour and aroma profile, though there are hundreds of different constituents too numerous to detail here, how can you accurately analyse these aromas and flavours in practice?

Cupping is a method designed to accurately assess the flavour, taste and aroma of various coffee beans so that roasters and coffee professionals can judge their relative merits and make buying decisions. It is the best way to gauge the complete profile of a particular bean, without the differentiation in flavour, aroma and mouthfeel that the brewing process brings. The differences among beans can often be minor, so it is important to be able to taste them side by side under consistent conditions to make sure that any differences in the cup are derived from the bean alone.

There are a number of stringent protocols in place to ensure consistency during the cupping assessment. A 170- to 255-gram (6- to 9-oz) cup is used, with about 7 to 8 grams of coffee in 150 millilitres (⅔ cup) of water. Various coffee samples are lightly roasted and then coarsely ground, similar to the level of grind used in a French press (see page 81). The coffee should have been roasted within the previous twenty-four hours but needs at least eight hours' rest after roasting. Once the coffee beans reach room temperature, they should be stored in airtight containers to minimize air exposure. The coffee should be ground immediately before cupping starts and left for no longer than fifteen minutes prior to cupping.

The water used should be clean and fresh and heated to 93 to 95°C (200 to 203°F), then the coffee is steeped in it for three to five minutes. The grounds will rise to the surface of the cup, forming a crust, which keeps some of the coffee aromas in the cup; once steeping is complete, a clean spoon should be used to break the crust. With your nose close to the cup, immediately breathe in the aromatics, evaluating and analysing their various qualities.

For tasting, which is the next stage of cupping, the grounds should be scooped off the top. Although the methods are different, the analysis in coffee tasting is as in-depth as it is in wine tasting. A spoonful of coffee is taken and slurped up while inhaling so that the full effect of both the taste and the aromas is experienced. The spoon is rinsed in a glass of clean water, and the next sample is tried in the same fashion. When cupping, it is important to compare aroma, body, sweetness, aftertaste, balance, acidity and any other characteristics of a particular bean. After tasting, it is common to then view the roasted bean in its whole state so that its appearance can be assessed; the bean is normally concealed until after cupping is completed so that visual judgements do not bias the tasting.

THE DECAFFEINATED OPTION

Although the presence of caffeine undeniably adds to the positive effects of coffee consumption, there are, as detailed earlier (see pages 36–41), many other bioavailable (readily metabolized) chemical compounds in coffee that can be beneficial to health.

Decaf is the ideal solution for coffee lovers who need to avoid caffeine consumption altogether, such as those with a high sensitivity to caffeine or those for whom avoidance is advisable in certain situations. The negative effects that caffeine can cause include insomnia, restlessness, nervousness, anxiety, increased heart rate and respiration, and muscle tremors. While some people can easily drink coffee after dinner and have no problems sleeping, many experience insomnia from the effects of caffeine if consumed just before bedtime. With decaffeinated coffee, the coffee experience can still be enjoyed but without the risk of interfering with sleep.

There are four main methods for decaffeinating coffee – two using solvents, one with carbon dioxide and one using water – however, the basic processes involved in all four methods have their similarities.

SOLVENT METHODS

In the direct variant, the coffee beans are first steamed for thirty minutes and then rinsed repeatedly over several hours with the liquid solvent ethyl acetate or methylene chloride, a process in which the solvent selectively binds to the caffeine molecules. The beans are removed and steamed again to remove the residual solvent and caffeine.

In the indirect variant, the beans are soaked for several hours in hot water, removing not only the caffeine but also the oils and flavours. The beans are then separated from the water and the solvent is added to the water, again binding to the caffeine. The solvent solution is heated to evaporate the solvent and caffeine together. The water remaining is reused to process fresh batches of beans, but the beans and water now have the same balance of coffee oils and flavours. The soaking

DECAFFEINATION METHODS

DIRECT SOLVENT

Beans are steamed   Solvent is added   Beans are steamed again

INDIRECT SOLVENT

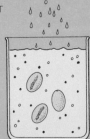
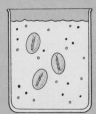

Beans are soaked   Solvent is added

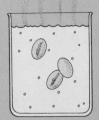
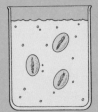

Solvent and caffeine
evaporate

Fresh beans are added
to the water

process now removes only the caffeine from the beans, which is then once more extracted by the solvent. In both variants of this method, the treated beans are dried back to the ideal moisture content and are then ready for processing in the same way as regular caffeinated coffee.

CARBON DIOXIDE METHOD

The beans are soaked in hot water in order to open their pores and mobilize the caffeine molecule. Carbon dioxide is then added to the water, creating sparkling water. The carbon dioxide attracts the mobilized caffeine molecules, removing them from the beans. There is a higher start-up cost in terms of investment in equipment with this method, so it is largely reserved for larger-batch processing.

SWISS WATER METHOD

In the 1980s, Swiss scientists devised a way to remove most of the caffeine from coffee beans without the use of any solvent or other additional products. Because this method proved commercially viable, it could be used for large-scale decaffeinated coffee production.

This method again starts with the coffee beans being soaked for many hours in hot water, leaching out the caffeine but also other important constituents of the coffee bean, such as oils and flavour molecules, so these need to be reabsorbed from the water but with the caffeine removed. To do this, the water is passed through an activated charcoal filter with a pore size designed to capture the larger caffeine molecules, while allowing the smaller flavour molecules to pass through and remain in the water. The beans are then returned to the filtered water to reabsorb the flavour molecules before processing is continued.

This form of decaffeination is relatively expensive because the caffeine cannot be recovered from the carbon filter, unlike in the solvent method, where the caffeine can be extracted and sold to companies that produce health foods, dietary supplements and soft drinks. This revenue offsets the cost of the decaffeination process.

DECAFFEINATION METHODS

CARBON DIOXIDE

Beans are soaked

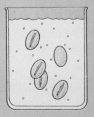

Carbon dioxide is added

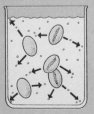

Carbon dioxide
attracts the caffeine

SWISS WATER

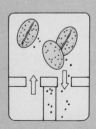

Beans are soaked, caffeine
leaches out

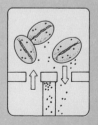

Water is passed through
a charcoal filter

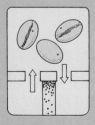

Beans are returned
to the water

THE ROLE OF MILK

How does cold, liquid milk turn into that creamy, frothy product of the steam wand? Basically, the denaturing of the proteins and lipids contained in milk that occurs during the heating process allows them to bond together. This creates a network that traps the air bubbles introduced by the steam wand, resulting in the foamy milk enjoyed in espresso coffees worldwide.

Adding milk to coffee changes its nutrient content significantly and can also counteract some of the negative effects coffee may have on human health, such as the possible increased risk of osteoporosis caused by drinking caffeinated beverages. Studies carried out on postmenopausal women showed that decreased bone mineral density was offset by consuming the equivalent of two cups of coffee with milk a day,[9] although another study showed that milk may impair absorption of the polyphenols and antioxidants in coffee, affecting the bioavailability of chlorogenic acids and its metabolites.[10] However, milk alone provides many health benefits, because it is a complete protein and a good dietary source of other nutrients, such as calcium and the B vitamins.

There are three major constituents of milk that are important to understand in regard to its flavour and frothing capability, and how milk interacts with coffee.

FATS

Fats are an important part of the content of milk, giving it a rounded mouthfeel. Milks with a higher fat content generally result in a fuller flavour and a richer, silkier beverage. Milk can be purchased with varying levels of milk fat: from fat-free milk (also called skimmed or non-fat milk), with less than 0.2 per cent; to low-fat or reduced-fat

[9] Barrett-Connor, E., Chun Chang, J., and Edelstein, S. 1994. 'Coffee-Associated Osteoporosis Offset by Daily Milk Consumption: The Rancho Bernardo Study.' *The Journal of the American Medical Association* 271 (4): 280–283

[10] Duarte, G. and Farah, A. 2011. 'Effect of simultaneous consumption of milk and coffee on chlorogenic acids' bioavailability in humans.' *Journal of Agricultural and Food Chemistry* 59 (14): 7925–7931

milk; with about 1 per cent and 2 per cent milk fat respectively; to whole milk, with about 3.25 to 3.5 per cent milk fat. Lower-fat milks generally create more foam, because there is less fat to compete with the proteins. However, once the fat content rises above whole milk level – for example single cream, which contains 18 per cent milk fat – foaming capability rises again. This explains why the higher the fat content in cream, the easier it is to whip.

PROTEINS

It is the proteins in milk that are largely responsible for foaming; as the milk heats to more than 60°C (140°F), these proteins denature, coating and stabilizing the air bubbles that are being introduced by the steam wand.

LACTOSE

Lactose, also known as milk sugar, is what gives milk its sweetness. Because lactose is less soluble than sucrose, it seems less sweet, but heating milk increases its solubility, breaking down the sugars and, therefore, increasing the sweetness of the milk.

Non-dairy milks can often react unpredictably in coffee. The extraction methods used in producing soy and nut milks can result in a low lipid content, and lipids are necessary for holding the air bubbles in the liquid. There is also a risk of the acids in the coffee coagulating the proteins in non-dairy milk if it is added cold to hot coffee. While many non-dairy milk products now contain stabilizers to reduce this risk, it is advisable to warm homemade or natural shop-bought non-dairy milks before adding to coffee or to let the coffee cool slightly before combining. A number of methods can prevent these milks from curdling, such as making sure not to overheat them or adding the coffee to the milk as you stir instead of the other way around.

HOW TO FROTH

1 Start with milk of your chosen fat content, taken straight from the refrigerator – it must be chilled. Make sure the milk is fresh – the older it is, the harder it will be to get proper foam. Pour the milk into a frothing jug until it reaches the bottom of the pouring spout; this will allow ample room in the jug for the milk to froth without spilling.

2 Insert the steam wand just below the surface of the milk on a slight angle, forcing the milk to move around in a whirlpool motion. This is called 'stretching' the milk, creating microfoam (tight air bubbles and silky foam) by letting air into the milk gently. It should make a hissing sound. Place your hand on the outside of the jug, and when the milk has almost reached body temperature, you want to stop introducing air, so change the position of the steam wand, moving it a fraction further into the jug. This will texture the milk, increasing the temperature without introducing more air.

3 Continue spinning the milk in a whirlpool motion, but with the steam wand slightly more submerged – you should no longer hear any hissing. The key to frothing the milk correctly is to tilt the jug slightly, texturing the milk until the jug becomes just too hot to touch, about 60°C (140°F).

4 Once the milk has been heated and frothed, tap the jug on the counter to pop any large bubbles. Let the milk rest while you prepare the espresso shots, then when you are ready to pour, swirl the milk around the jug to make sure it is even in consistency, tapping it on the counter again if there are any large bubbles remaining. The milk should be smooth and shiny, resembling wet paint.

FROTHING MILK

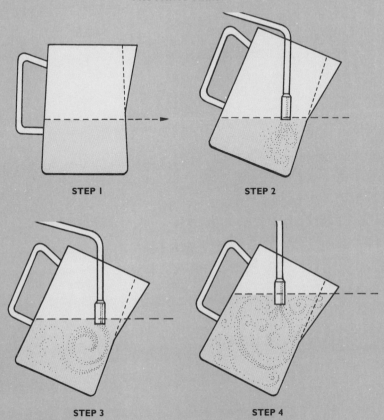

STEP 1

STEP 2

STEP 3

STEP 4

'The hotter your milk, the sweeter it becomes – up to a point. Lactose (the sweet part of milk) is perceived as five times less sweet than regular sugar. Heating milk up increases lactose's solubility and hence the sweetness you taste. Aim for milk around the 58 to 60°C (136 to 140°F) mark. Above that, you start to denature the milk proteins and create lower-quality foam.'

MATTHEW PERGER
WORLD CHAMPION BARISTA, ST ALI & SENSORY LAB, AUSTRALIA

Roast & Grind

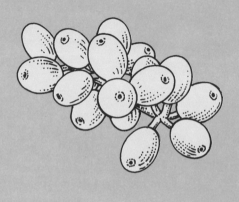

ROAST & GRIND THE GREEN BEAN

The processed green coffee bean is usually exported in its unroasted state because it is less prone to deterioration than its roasted counterpart, but environmental and other factors can all too easily impact the quality of the end coffee product.

Green coffee beans remain in a fairly stable condition if stored in a cool, dry place and will not start to deteriorate for twelve months or more. Ideally, the beans should retain the 10 to 12 per cent moisture content achieved in the final stage of processing until the moment roasting begins, but less than ideal temperature and humidity levels can often cause moisture absorption or additional drying, resulting in a reduction in the quality of the beans. The optimum temperature in which to store green coffee beans varies greatly according to different sources, but most agree that the beans should remain in relatively cool conditions, and no higher than 20 to 25°C (68 to 77°F).

During transportation, and shipping in particular, coffee beans can be subjected to huge fluctuations in temperature and air humidity, with condensation being the probable outcome. Condensation is a major enemy of coffee exporters, because it can lead to the growth of mould and the destruction of coffee flavours – and at worst, irreparable damage to the entire shipment. Even if they are dried to the safer end of the requisite moisture level during processing (that is, less than 12 per cent), adverse environmental conditions can nevertheless cause the green beans to absorb enough moisture for mould to grow.

The roasted bean, by contrast, is much less robust and can start to develop a stale aroma and flavour only two weeks after roasting, as the lipids present in the bean oxidize. For optimum flavour and freshness, roasted coffee should be consumed before this process begins, having been safely protected from air, moisture, heat and light (see page 74).

Most people assume that green coffee beans are unpalatable until roasted, but different cultures have long been brewing or using green coffee beans in a variety of ways.

Green coffee beans are one of the richest dietary sources of chlorogenic acids, which are highly effective plant-based antioxidants. Furthermore, studies have shown that these chlorogenic acids are also highly bioavailable – in other words, they are easily metabolized by the human body.[1] For this reason, green coffee extract has been used extensively in nutraceuticals – various nutritional products and dietary supplements purported to provide health benefits. Green beans are currently touted as a treatment or aid for everything from heart health to weight loss, and while these beans may not exactly be the 'miracle cure' they are claimed to be, they have been proven to provide some certain health benefits.

Some human studies have indicated that green coffee bean extract may reduce hypertension,[2] and other human and animal studies suggest that it holds promise in helping combat excess weight and diabetes.[3] Certain trials have shown that green coffee extract can help reduce the weight of pre-obese adults and prevent obesity in overweight adults; others have linked coffee consumption with a decreased risk of type 2 diabetes. While these claims are yet to be validated by in-depth studies, it cannot be denied that the potentially beneficial chemicals and compounds found in coffee beans are present in higher concentrations when in their unroasted state.

[1] Farah, A., Monteiro, M., Donangelo, C. M., and Lafay, S. 2008. 'Biochemical, Molecular and Genetic Mechanisms: Chlorogenic Acids from Green Coffee Extract are Highly Bioavailable in Humans.' *The Journal of Nutrition* 138 (12): 2309–2315

[2] Watanabe, T., Arai, Y., Mitsui, Y., Kusuara, T., Okawa, W., Kajihara, and Y., Saito I. 2006. 'The blood pressure-lowering effect and safety of chlorogenic acid from green coffee bean extract in essential hypertension.' *Clinical and Experimental Hypertension* 28 (5): 439–449

[3] Vinson, J., Burnham, B., and Nagendran, M. 2012. 'Randomized, double-blind, placebo-controlled, linear dose, crossover study to evaluate the efficacy and safety of a green coffee bean extract in overweight subjects.' *Diabetes, Metabolic Syndrome, and Obesity: Targets and Therapy* , 5, 21–27

SPOTTING DEFECTS

You can buy green coffee beans for roasting at home so that you can create a coffee tailored to your own tastes and specifications. However, to make sure that you start with a good-quality product, you need to know how to recognize defects in the unroasted bean.

A number of defects can be found in green coffee beans as a result of problems or faults occurring in the various stages of growth, harvesting or processing. Some of the more important ones to look for are detailed below.

FULL/PARTIAL BLACK As the term indicates, these beans are black and opaque, and they impart a rotted fruit, sour, mouldy or dirty flavour. They are classed as full black if more than half the bean is affected, or partial if less than half is affected. This defect is caused by overfermentation due to overripe fruit or substandard processing conditions.

FULL/PARTIAL SOUR These beans are yellowish/red/brown and impart a vinegary, sour flavour. The bean is classed full sour if more than half is affected, or partial if less than half is affected. This is one of the worst defects to occur in coffee beans, because a single full sour is thought to have the ability to contaminate an entire pot of coffee.

STINKERS When broken open, these beans produce a rotten smell with a flavour to match, usually indicating bacteria or mould contamination that may be caused by overfermentation. These beans have the potential to infect and contaminate a whole batch of beans, leading to the ruination of a large quantity of 'healthy' coffee. Unfortunately, this type of defective bean is one of the most difficult to detect, because it usually looks normal in external appearance.

STICKS/STONES It is regarded as a batch defect when a consignment of green coffee beans is found to contain large- or medium-size foreign objects, such as sticks or stones.

POD/CHERRY If a bean makes it through to the final stage with the fruit, or 'cherry', still attached, the batch is considered defective; this could be due to improperly maintained or adjusted machinery.

PARCHMENT Similarly, improperly maintained or adjusted machinery can result in the parchment layer remaining attached to the fully processed bean.

HULL Again, improperly maintained or adjusted machinery can cause traces of dried pulp to remain attached to the fully processed bean.

INSECT DAMAGE These beans exhibit marks or holes where insects have bored into the fruit, laying eggs inside that develop into larvae. The affected beans can impart a dirty, mouldy or sour flavour.

WITHERED (QUAKERS) Small beans with a wrinkled, raisinlike appearance are the result of a water deficiency in the fruits' development. They impart a grassy flavour when present in sufficient quantities and do not darken as much as others when roasting.

GRADING

There is no single, universally adopted international grading and classification system for green coffee, although many countries defer to the protocols detailed by the Specialty Coffee Association of America Green Arabica Coffee Classification System (SCAA GACCS). This takes into account the correlation between cup quality and defective beans, but because of the vast number of factors that need to be taken into consideration it is still not a perfect system.

Although grading protocols vary among different countries, most take into account aspects of the following when determining the grade of a bean: its botanical variety, the region and the altitude in which the bean was grown, the method of processing, size, shape, colour, density, defects and cup quality.

ROASTING

Roasting is a vital part of the coffee production process – it increases the chemical complexity of the beans substantially, thereby unlocking their aromas and flavours.

During the high-temperature roasting process, a number of chemical reactions take place. In what is known as the Maillard reaction, aromatic molecular compounds develop through the combination or destruction of amino acids, sugars, peptides and proteins, which gives coffee its dominant flavours. Green coffee contains about two hundred and fifty aromatic molecular compounds, but through roasting that figure increases to more than eight hundred.

ROASTING EFFECTS

During the roasting process, the coffee bean goes through its most drastic colour changes. Starting out as a particular shade of green, the first colour change that the bean undergoes is a paling as it loses steam. The green colour eventually pales to a yellow as the coffee bean heats up and heads towards the first crack. The yellow starts to take on the first hints of brown as the initial toasty aromatic notes start to develop. As the bean gets browner, it starts to expand ever so slightly. This is when the Maillard reaction takes place. The light brown stage leads to the first crack, where the colour is still uneven and the chaff (waste) is significantly reduced.

After the first crack has finished, the bean will have expanded and the colour starts to even out. It is a medium brown at this stage, and it will now continue to get darker as it heads towards the second crack. As the second crack draws nearer, a faint sheen of oil starts to appear on the surface of the bean as the coffee oils are released. At this stage, the bean will have prominent roasted flavours and be dark.

The bean can be taken all the way to a dark roast, where all the sugars are caramelized and a carbon or ashy flavour starts to take hold, but many of the nuances of the bean flavour will be lost at this point.

THE MAILLARD REACTION

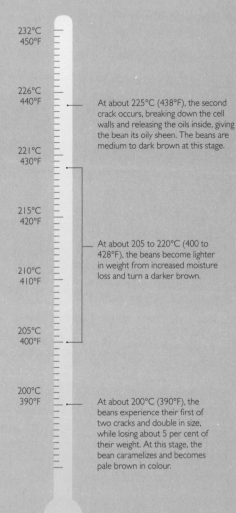

232°C
450°F

226°C
440°F

At about 225°C (438°F), the second crack occurs, breaking down the cell walls and releasing the oils inside, giving the bean its oily sheen. The beans are medium to dark brown at this stage.

221°C
430°F

215°C
420°F

At about 205 to 220°C (400 to 428°F), the beans become lighter in weight from increased moisture loss and turn a darker brown.

210°C
410°F

205°C
400°F

200°C
390°F

At about 200°C (390°F), the beans experience their first of two cracks and double in size, while losing about 5 per cent of their weight. At this stage, the bean caramelizes and becomes pale brown in colour.

As the green coffee beans heat up, they begin to toast and smell like popcorn, slowly turning yellow.

EUROPEAN & THIRD WAVE ROASTING

For a traditional European roast, the roasting process is halted somewhere between the end of the first crack and midway through the second crack, depending on what level of roast is required for the intended flavour profile. Arabica and Robusta beans need different roasting times, and the longer the roasting time, the deeper and more intense the flavours will be.

The Third Wave Coffee movement has been experimenting with new roasting methods, developing a style very different from that of the traditional European roast. However, the machinery and actual roasting processes do not differ greatly; it is the level to which the Third Wave Coffee roasters roast their beans that sets the two approaches apart.

The term 'Third Wave Coffee' was coined around the turn of the millennium, soon after the first influx of artisanal coffee bars started cropping up around the United States in the 1990s. The 'First Wave' refers to the initial introduction of coffee in ground and instant varieties into homes worldwide, and the 'Second Wave' is the proliferation of espresso machines and global coffee giants such as Starbucks. The Third Wave Coffee movement is a modern ideal that aims to bring coffee production and consumption in line with the artisanal food movement. It focuses on providing high-quality, artisanal coffee for those who value the bean on its own merits, not merely as a caffeine delivery system or a beverage to which you add sweeteners or milk. Those involved in the movement source their beans from individual farms, take note of processing methods, varietals and region, and employ highly skilled and qualified individuals who passionately dedicate themselves to bringing out the best from every coffee bean. The Third Wave Coffee movement is known for especially light roasting. Regardless of the bean, Third Wave Coffee roasters often roast only until just after the first crack. The roasted beans range from pale to medium brown and do not exhibit that dark, shiny exterior characteristic of traditional European roasts.

While traditional roasters are focused on the flavours developed through the roasting process itself, those of the Third Wave Coffee movement are predominantly concerned with the fundamental flavours that derive from the coffee plant varietal, its origin and the terroir. They concentrate their efforts on blending and roasting to bring out and accentuate these unique, intrinsic flavours. Third Wave Coffee roasters often comment that the flavours produced by darker roasts overwhelm the subtle differences among varietals, making darker roasted coffees taste more uniform, and they contend that the higher the grade of bean, the lighter the roast should be, because there is little point in roasting away the fine nuances of a premium-grade bean. Many roasters believe that darker roasts can create a bitter brew and that beans roasted to the second crack have ashy, carbon-like flavours.

These two divergent schools of coffee roasting thought can, however, produce roasted coffee of an equally high quality – the choice simply depends on the individual consumer's flavour preference.

STYLES OF ROAST

Varieties of roast style have evolved over time and taken on specific names, sometimes that of the country in which they are especially popular. Traditional Italian and French roasts, for example, are generally dark, whereas medium roasts are often known as American roasts, because this level of roasting is most favoured in the United States.

While certain books, websites and coffee companies may tell you that there are a limited number of possible roasts, the truth of the matter is that there are dozens of different combinations. Roast styles are frequently classed by colour, but the type of bean in question often plays a large part in determining how the final roast colour will actually appear. Dry-processed coffees, for instance, will not generally roast to a single uniform colour, making visual analysis of the roast problematic. The various varietals and coffees from different origins exhibit their own distinct aromatic and visual characteristics during roasting. For example, Sumatran beans can be misleading, often appearing pale when they are actually at a much darker roast than their appearance indicates.

Various coffee beans roast at different speeds and temperatures, exhibiting distinct aromatic and visual characteristics at certain stages of the process. Roasters aim for different temperatures and results for the same beans, roasting them to their own and their customers' personal preferences.

So although the roast colour can give you a rough idea of roast style, identification on a visual basis alone is not always an accurate guide. As a general rule, a better way of judging roast level is to inspect the appearance of the bean – the shinier the bean, the more prominent the roast flavours will be. Dull beans will have been roasted only up to or just beyond the first crack stage, whereas especially shiny beans have been roasted up to or beyond the second crack stage, when rich roast flavours develop.

ROAST COLOUR	APPEARANCE	COMMON NAMES	FLAVOUR PROFILE
Pale	Dry	Cinnamon	Especially light-bodied; flavours of origin prominent, roasting flavours have not begun to develop.
Pale-Medium	Dry	American Regular	Sugars begin to caramelize and more body starts to develop. This stage is the preferred roast level for Third Wave Coffee roasters. Origin character is particularly prominent.
Medium	Dry/ oily patches	American Breakfast	Origin character is prominent; cup is full-bodied with rich caramelization.
Medium-Dark	Becoming shiny	City Full City Vienna	Second crack occurs, and roasting flavours start to match or overtake original flavours. Considered a generic roast, many beans for non-premium uses are roasted to this level.
Dark	Shiny	Continental European Italian French	Flavours generated from roasting dominate; they have lost much of their acidity, and body will become lighter as aromatic compounds are released.

ROASTING MACHINES

To roast coffee beans according to the specifications in the table on page 63, a certain amount of speciality equipment is required. Roasting machines come in a multitude of sizes, all of which are constructed on the same basic principles, including: a flame to heat up the environment or air surrounding the beans, controlled at all times by a coffee roaster that ensures the temperature remains constant; a drum or hot-air bed that rotates the beans so they evenly roast; and a drier to cool the beans immediately after being removed from the roaster, to halt the cooking process.

There are two main kinds of coffee roaster: drum-style machines that rotate and tumble the beans around in a hot environment, and hot-air roasters that tumble the coffee beans while hot air is blown through the perforated bed they are resting on. Both of these machines are generally fairly large, capable of roasting large batches of green coffee beans. Small roasters are commonly used to roast and test small batches of beans, and these are also popular with coffee aficionados who are eager to experiment with roasting their own coffee at home.

'Lighter roasts are best for drip/filter/French press, etc.
Darker roasts are usually reserved for espresso
and stovetop/macchinetta.'

MATTHEW PERGER
WORLD CHAMPION BARISTA, ST ALI AND SENSORY LAB, AUSTRALIA

COFFEE ROASTERS

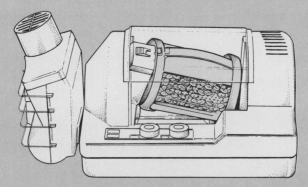

Drum roaster

Hot-air roaster

GRINDING

Many say that a grinder is one of the most important pieces of equipment for making coffee. A poor-quality grinder can be seriously detrimental to your coffee; it is vital to purchase one that is capable of producing an even grind.

There are two main types of coffee grinder: the blade and the burr grinder. Whereas the blade grinder spins and chops the beans into tiny pieces, the burr grinder truly grinds, allowing a fuller unlocking of the chemical compounds stored within the bean. However, some people are of the opinion that beans ground with a burr grinder often taste bitter, possibly due to the greater surface area of coffee coming into contact with the water during brewing.

BLADE GRINDERS These grinders are inexpensive, but you need to know what your required grind level should look like when using them. The longer you grind, the finer the grind will be, so a combination of timing and keeping an eye on the texture is the only way of gauging the level of grind suitable for your chosen brewing method. Because blade grinders chop instead of pulverize, they often produce an uneven grind, making for a less smooth extraction. Blade grinders cannot generally grind finely enough for espresso or Turkish coffee.

Blade grinder

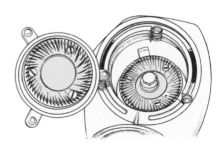

Burr grinder

BURR GRINDERS Unlike blade grinders, burr grinders can grind coffee for any purpose. The width between the burrs into which the coffee beans fall and are pulverized to a consistent size can be varied and set as required. This is especially important for espresso, because uneven grounds can cause water to channel unevenly through the coffee packed into the portafilter, overextracting and possibly burning some grounds while underextracting the remainder.

The temperature of the beans is another important factor in retaining their flavour profile. The oils and aromas can easily dissipate if the beans become too hot during grinding, although most grinders will not heat the beans to a high enough temperature to risk this occurring.

Beans should always be freshly ground, because the oils and aromas unlocked from the grinding process degrade quickly, usually within fifteen minutes after grinding.

LEVELS OF GRIND & BREWING METHODS

The method and extent to which the coffee bean is ground has a substantial effect on the caffeine content of the final beverage. A finer grind means that a larger surface area comes into contact with water, allowing a more complete caffeine extraction.

Different levels of grind can be chosen to make sure that you unlock the optimum flavour in your preferred brewing method. The panel on page 68 provides a rough guide to the ideal level of grind for the various methods of brewing. However, some machines and equipment require particular types of grind, so make sure you check the manufacturer's directions for additional guidance.

While many baristas determine whether the grind is correct by touch and sight, they will generally make adjustments according to the speed at which the coffee is extracted by the espresso machine. The coffee dosage will be weighed and the extraction timed, and if they are not within the correct range, the grind will be adjusted.

THE SEVEN PRIMARY LEVELS OF GRIND

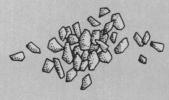

EXTRA-COARSE
Cold brew

COARSE
French press, cupping

MEDIUM-COARSE
Chemex

MEDIUM
Drip or filter

MEDIUM-FINE
Pour-over, siphon/vacuum

FINE
Espresso, AeroPress

EXTRA-FINE
Turkish

When grinding for espresso at home, as a rule of thumb if the coffee is coming out too fast, use a finer grind to slow down the extraction; or, if the coffee is coming out too slowly, make the grind coarser.

If your coffee tastes a little sour, this is often due to underextraction. With methods of brewing other than espresso, using a finer grind will allow more coffee to be extracted during the brewing time. The same is true of bitter coffee – this could be due to your beans, equipment or brewing method, but it may also be caused by overextraction. Make the grounds a little coarser and to slow down the extraction rate.

Environmental conditions can also have a bearing on the level of grind. Varying temperatures and humidity levels can cause the beans to react differently, requiring an adjustment in the level of grind accordingly. This is because coffee is hydroscopic – that is, it readily draws moisture from the air – resulting in swelling of the beans, which can mean that the coffee is more tightly packed in the portafilter, reducing flow rate and potentially leading to overextraction. This is one of the main reasons that coffee shops need to recalibrate their machines every morning, and the home barista may also need to adjust the grind daily, depending on the environmental conditions. Just keep an eye on your morning brew, and if any issues arise, use this section to troubleshoot and adjust your grind size.

DO-IT-YOURSELF

For many people, do-it-yourself, or 'from scratch', food processing is not only interesting and enjoyable but also allows for individualization. Coffee is no different, and there is much to experiment with in making your own varieties or styles of coffee.

The recent artisanal food movement has brought food quality and awareness of food production into the mainstream, with increasingly more people becoming interested in being actively involved with producing their food. Whether a coffee lover owns a French press or macchinetta, or is a high-end connoisseur with everything from a hand-powered piston espresso machine to a top-of-the-line burr grinder, public interest in coffee production is increasing at a rapid rate.

For anyone who makes coffee at home, there is always a certain do-it-yourself aspect to it. Many freshly brew their coffee daily, but what about those who want to take this a step further? How else can you, as a consumer, fine-tune your morning brew to your exact specification?

It is perfectly possible to roast your own coffee beans at home, allowing you to make finely tuned adjustments to every aspect of your brew. However, first you need to purchase green (unroasted) coffee beans. There are several reliable online sources and a simple web search will turn up the leading suppliers, but the beans will still need careful selection (pages 55–59 give guidance on how to identify bean defects and select the highest grade). Once you have selected and purchased your batch of green beans, the next stage is to decide what level of roast you want to start with (see pages 62–63). For premium-grade Arabica with distinct origin characteristics, for example, try a lighter roast, or if you prefer stronger flavours, a darker roast may be more to your taste.

DIY ROASTING METHODS

There are a number of ways you can roast coffee beans at home, whether you are willing to invest in speciality equipment or you just want to try using regular domestic appliances. For example, the beans can be toasted on the hob in a frying pan, or you could purchase a professional small-batch sample roaster.

OVEN Oven roasting does not generally roast coffee particularly evenly, but it can create interesting flavours. Using a perforated baking tray such as a pizza pan, lay the coffee beans out in a single layer and preheat the oven to 260°C (500°F), using an external oven thermometer to check that it has reached the correct temperature. Place the tray on the middle rack and wait for about seven minutes for the beans to reach first crack stage (see page 60). You will hear this happen in a similar way to popcorn.

After the first crack, keep a close eye on the beans until they are just a little paler than the roast style you require; they will continue to roast after being removed from the oven before they cool, so be careful not to take them too close to your desired roast colour. In any case, do not let the beans roast for longer than twenty minutes, because this will result in a flat cup of coffee.

POPCORN POPPER There are dangers in using any heat or heated appliance at home, but this method could potentially be extra hazardous and, as such, cannot be recommended. However, if you do decide to roast coffee using a popcorn popper, a few safety precautions must be taken. The following information should not be taken as professional advice: putting it into practice is entirely at your own risk.

In essence, roasting coffee is similar to making popcorn, so a popcorn popper can improvise as a home coffee-roasting appliance. However, only specific types of popcorn popper may be suitable for roasting coffee. Do not use a machine that pushes hot air into the canister through mesh on the bottom – the chaff that flakes off the coffee

DIY ROASTING METHODS

Oven

Popcorn popper

Frying pan/hob

Sample roaster

beans can ignite and cause serious safety concerns. Find a popcorn maker with side vents that will push the chaff up and out so it can be collected in a bowl placed in front of the outlet.

Weigh out as many coffee beans as you would popcorn kernels and place them in the machine. The first crack should occur after about four minutes, and the machine should be turned off at the point when the coffee has almost reached your ideal roast style. Never leave the machine unattended during roasting. Once the roast is complete, remove the beans to a sieve and toss quickly to cool them.

FRYING PAN/HOB Using a frying pan is the old-school way of roasting coffee beans – simply placing them in the pan over a heat source and tossing them to even out the roast. This method generally produces the lowest cup quality and requires the most effort, and you must be careful to prevent burns. Heat up the frying pan to 260°C (500°F) – place an oven thermometer inside to check that it has reached the correct temperature. Place the beans in the pan, cover with a lid and shake, keeping the beans in motion for the entire roasting process, which should take about five minutes; any pauses will result in an uneven roast. As with the previous methods, remove the pan from the heat when the beans are slightly paler in colour than required and immediately toss in a sieve to cool.

SAMPLE ROASTER Coffee roasting companies need to test-roast a small batch of beans before using their large commercial roasters, which require a substantial minimum capacity to operate. To prevent waste while they determine the perfect roast for a certain type of bean, they use small sample roasters, and these can be purchased for do-it-yourself coffee roasting. Because they are professional-grade roasters, they will accurately and evenly roast your coffee.

STORAGE

As with all other food products, the environment in which you store your coffee beans has a huge effect on the flavour, aroma and mouthfeel of your brew. The major factors that need to be controlled are air, moisture, heat and light.

Air exposure is perhaps the easiest way for your beans to deteriorate. It is recommended that, after purchasing a batch of beans, you store a small quantity separately in a canister as a daily supply. The bulk of the beans should be stored in a large canister, from which you top off the smaller container when it is empty. This reduces the number of times that the beans are exposed to oxygen, greatly slowing deterioration. Ideally, coffee beans should not be stored in paper, because paper allows airflow; heavy-duty foil or plastic are better alternatives for excluding air.

Moisture also needs to be controlled to keep your beans in prime condition. When the roasted bean is exposed to moisture, it can be ruined almost immediately, and fungal contamination can occur. It is not simply dampness or humidity that you need to be aware of in guarding against the threat of moisture; significant changes in temperature can cause condensation. For this reason, you should not store your coffee beans in the refrigerator or freezer.

Some sources state that refrigeration preserves the coffee bean, ensuring freshness, but it is actually detrimental. If whole coffee beans must be purchased in bulk, as a last resort they can be stored in the freezer for up to a month in airtight bags, removing as much air as possible. Protecting the beans from light is less of an issue in this case, because the freezer provides a dark environment.

Protecting your coffee beans from heat is often harder than it seems. If you live in a location where the temperature fluctuates, you simply cannot be sure that your beans are stored at a constant temperature. The best advice is to find the coolest place in your house – at the back of a cupboard and as low to the ground as possible, making sure there is no heat source or anything that may cause the temperature to fluctuate, such as a hot-water pipe or sink drainage, nearby. The storage place should also be dark to protect the beans from the harmful effects of light.

Coffee starts to lose its freshness soon after roasting, so it is important to purchase freshly roasted beans and use them within one to two weeks. An easy way to tell how fresh coffee beans are is simply by looking at the package and checking for a valve. Coffee emits carbon dioxide after roasting, so a valve allows gases to escape and prevents the bag from popping. To vacuum-seal coffee, it needs to have released all of its carbon dioxide, so it is left to rest before bagging. Consequently, the vacuum sealing preserves coffee longer during transportation and sitting on the supermarket shelf, but the product may not have been at its peak when packaged. The safest solution is to purchase from local roasters in small quantities so that you can be assured that the beans are fresh.

Coffee should always be purchased and stored as whole beans. You can source the finest premium or specialty coffee, but if it is pre-ground, your cup will never be able to attain the flavour of freshly ground beans. Grind what you require only as you need it, and store the remainder of the beans whole in airtight glass or ceramic containers in a cool, dark place.

INSTANT COFFEE

Instant coffee is made from roasted and ground coffee that is brewed in a similar way to percolation but is highly concentrated. There are then two different methods of creating the gritty powder that can be reconstituted immediately in the cup.

The extracted coffee can be spray-dried or freeze-dried, whichever method is used determining the consistency of the product. Both of these methods remove the liquids by drying, leaving behind only the coffee solids. Spray-drying consists of misting the brew into dry, hot air, evaporating the liquids, and leaving a fine coffee powder at the bottom of the machine. Sometimes this powder is collected and pressed into granules for dosing; otherwise, it is packaged as is in fine powder form. Freeze-drying involves freezing the extracted coffee and then placing it in a vacuum and extracting the liquids. Cut into granules, the coffee is subsequently packaged and shipped. Some studies have shown that of the two methods, freeze-drying retains more coffee flavour.[4]

While instant coffee often gets a bad rap, the concentration that occurs during the extraction process is said to lead to a higher antioxidant content than freshly brewed coffee. However, due to the ratio of water to coffee in traditional preparation methods, instant and regular ground coffee have similar antioxidant levels. In essence, a cup of instant is comparable to a cup of percolated coffee, with all the flavours and aromas being preserved by drying.

The negative view of instant coffee may be largely attributed to the fact that, because it is perceived as a low-value product, poor-quality beans are often used and so, regardless of the method of brewing, the base ingredient is incapable of yielding a good brew. Various coffee brands will every now and then try to push an instant coffee line, but it remains a tough challenge in many markets for the product to shake off its downbeat image.

[4] Muller, P. G. (1990). *North American Food Processing Technologies*. Ottawa: Inter-American Institute for Cooperation on Agriculture.

SPRAY DRYING

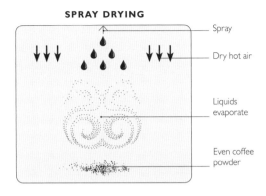

Spray

Dry hot air

Liquids evaporate

Even coffee powder

FREEZE DRYING

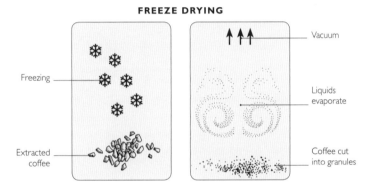

Freezing

Extracted coffee

Vacuum

Liquids evaporate

Coffee cut into granules

Some countries have a more positive view of instant coffee, such as the UK, where brands that use premium and/or all Arabica beans are available and, therefore, the quality is of a higher standard. Sales of instant coffee accounted for just over 80 per cent of the UK take-home coffee market in 2012,[5] and some brands of instant coffee actually cost more per cup than that brewed from ground coffee. As with all coffee consumption, you need to be a discerning consumer and figure out what you want from your daily brew and by which means that is best delivered.

[5] Mintel Business Market Research Report on Coffee – UK, April 2012

Brewing, Extraction & Balance

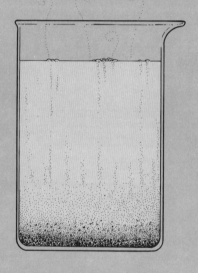

BREWING METHODS

The long history and global popularity of coffee has spawned hundreds of methods of turning bean into beverage. Coffee has come a long way from the simple decoction made by heating water and grounds in a pot set over a campfire. The many types of appliances and machines all create slightly different brews, but, in essence, there are four main ways to extract coffee: filter, boil, pressure and steep.

DRIP OR FILTER

The basic method of coffee extraction involves pouring hot water over ground beans suspended in a filter. Various materials are used to filter out the grounds, from cloth to metal to paper. The water soaks through the grounds, extracting soluble fats, chemicals and aromas, and falls into a collection pot or cup. There are convenient and laborious ways of drip-brewing; the automatic drip coffee-maker is one popular, effortless option, but it is not known for making superior coffee. Third Wave Coffee connoisseurs have brought specialty drip-brew methods, such as the pour-over, into fashion (see page 128), with single-cup drip coffee becoming a favoured brewing method in speciality coffee bars and in homes.

Coffee brewed through a filter has fewer lipids than coffee prepared using other methods;[1] meaning that filter coffee contains fewer coffee oils than espresso. While fewer oils can make for a crisper cup, some prefer the thick, syrupy mouthfeel of those brews rich in oils. Coffee beans should be ground medium-fine for most filter-brewing methods, with the consistency of sand or granulated table salt.

TURKISH

A comparable method of brewing is used in Greece, Africa, the Middle East, Turkey and Russia, but it is usually referred to as Turkish coffee.

[1] Ratnayake, W., Hollywood, R., O'Grady, E., and Stavric, B. 1993. 'Lipid content and composition of coffee brews prepared by different methods.' *Food and Chemical Toxicology* 31 (4): 263–269

It consists of heating water with added ground coffee to just a boil in a special pot (see page 97) and then removing it from and returning it to the heat source in order to control the temperature until the coffee is extracted. It requires an especially fine grind level, even finer than that for espresso, which is only achievable by using a traditional Turkish hand coffee grinder or a good-quality burr grinder. This type of coffee is strong, and unless you are careful, can easily be overextracted.

PERCOLATOR

Percolated coffee is brewed in a coffeepot that is heated from below until the water is so hot it splashes up and is repeatedly forced through coffee grounds, seeping back into the bottom section of the pot as it cools (see page 104). During the extraction process, the coffee may become too hot as it brews; consequently it is easily overextracted unless the beans are coarsely ground. The coffee should be allowed to percolate only for about three minutes – otherwise it will develop a bitter and tarry taste.

ESPRESSO

Espresso is one of the mostly highly regarded coffee extraction methods. The various ways of brewing espresso all use the same principle: hot water is forced under pressure through finely ground coffee beans to extract a concentrated, flavourful and aromatic liquid – the shot.

Espresso coffee is prepared with finely ground beans, the exact grind level being fine-tuned according to the environment and flow rate to keep the shot from over- or underextracting. Any type of roast may be used – darker roasts are preferred in Italy, whereas American coffee producers often tend towards much lighter roasts.

The macchinetta (see page 100) is a simple way to brew espresso at home, and it is also a common method of preparing coffee in Italy. In this case, the coffee should be ground slightly coarser than for a traditional espresso grind, similar to that for drip coffee.

A more recent invention, the AeroPress, is a combination of espresso and the French press (see below), consisting of two cylinders and a fine paper filter. The filter is placed at the bottom of the larger cylinder and the coffee dosed on top. The second cylinder is plunged into the first, pressing the coffee into a cup. Said to deliver espresso-strength coffee, it is similar to filter coffee with less sediment than the French press due to the fine filter. The grind used is slightly finer than that used for espresso.

FRENCH PRESS

The French press, or *cafetière*, uses the steeping method of extraction. Coarsely ground coffee is steeped in hot water and, once brewing is complete, the plunger is pressed down, trapping the grounds under the filter. The press tends to leave a relatively large quantity of sediment, but a good-quality burr grinder will produce an even grind, thus reducing the amount of sediment that can pass through the filter. French press coffee needs to be consumed within about ten minutes of brewing; it will continue to extract even after it has been plunged because the grounds are still immersed in the liquid.

COLD BREW

Cold water is used in a few brewing methods, including the Toddy or Filtron brewing systems. The extraction is slow – up to twenty-four hours – and produces a thick, dark and strong liquid that is diluted with hot or cold water or milk. Coffee grounds are added with cold water to a brewing container fitted with a filter and a plug. After twelve hours of steeping, the plug is removed and the coffee filters into a pitcher below.

Cold brew coffee has low acidity levels, because certain oils and fatty acids are released only at high temperatures. However, lovers of espresso or French press coffees may find cold brew less flavourful: oils extracted at high heat make a discernible contribution to the flavour profile.

Because of the long extraction time, beans should be ground coarsely for this brewing method.

SOLUBILITY

The solubility of various flavour molecules is an important scientific principle to grasp, because it can help you understand the relationship between extraction and flavour. This will enable you to analyse your brew according to which flavours are present and to tweak your dosage and method until you achieve the ideal cup.

There are two main concepts involved in solubility, referred to in the industry as Total Dissolved Solids (TDS) and extraction yield.

TDS is expressed as a percentage, which tells you what proportion of your cup is dissolved coffee solids – that is, the strength of your coffee. A typical cup of coffee will consist of 1.20 to 1.45 per cent soluble coffee solids, the remainder being water. Espresso has a much higher TDS, because it is a much more concentrated form of coffee. A refractometer or brew strength meter can be purchased and used to measure the percentage of coffee solids present; levels that are too high or too low indicate overextraction or underextraction respectively.

The coffee bean itself is generally about 30 per cent soluble, and the remainder is largely made up of cellulose, which is insoluble during brewing. Extraction yield refers to the percentage of coffee material that has been removed from the grounds, and the ideal range is somewhere between 18 and 22 per cent of the soluble coffee material.

THE COFFEE BREWING CONTROL CHART

The coffee brewing control chart (opposite) is one of the most important tools you can use to achieve your ideal cup of coffee. In combination with a refractometer or brew strength meter, it enables you to scientifically adjust your dosage and method according to your unique specifications. Note that this chart is designed for use with only non-espresso brews, because espresso is a concentrated brew with much higher levels of solubles. The Specialty Coffee Association of America (SCAA) and The Speciality Coffee Association of Europe (SCAE) have slightly different ideal strengths.

Starting with a certain quantity of coffee in relation to 1 kilogram (1 litre/4¼ cups) of water – for example, 60 grams of coffee (⅔ cup) per 1 kilogram of water – brew a cup using your chosen brewing method, then use a refractometer or brew strength meter to determine the concentration of coffee solubles in your cup. Referring to the chart, follow the diagonal line down from 60 grams until you reach the percentage of coffee solubles as determined by your analysis, and then follow that point down vertically to determine the extraction. For example, 60 grams of coffee per liter is analysed as 1.10 per cent concentration. So following the diagonal line from 60 grams until it meets 1.10 per cent concentration, the vertical path then leads down to show a 16 per cent extraction. The chart has thus determined that this cup of coffee is 'weak' and 'underdeveloped' and that the extraction needs to be increased to bring the solubles yield to between 18 and 22 per cent, ideally closer to 20 per cent. To do this, the concentration of soluble coffee solids needs to be increased, which can be achieved by either decreasing the grind level or increasing the brew time – or both.

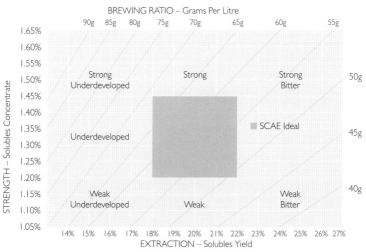

Chart courtesy of Speciality Coffee Association of Europe

EXTRACTION

Coffee is all about balance, and there are distinct stages of coffee extraction that create balanced flavours as different compounds are released. Removing or minimizing any of these stages affects the flavour profile.

Most people would assume that coffee that is too strong is also overdeveloped. This is a misconception: as the brewing chart on page 83 shows, coffee can be strong yet still underdeveloped. This is because the development of the brew refers to the flavour, not strength, and the different compounds that are released over the brewing cycle. As different solubles are extracted at different times, a lower extraction yield means that later-stage solubles have not had a chance to be extracted, resulting in underextraction and unbalanced flavours.

For example, the extraction yield of a regular cup of coffee might be measured to be 25 per cent. As such, it would be considered overextracted, because it contains too high a percentage of the available soluble material of the beans. An espresso shot, by comparison, might measure 17 per cent extraction yield, but, of course, the espresso

CREMA

Espresso brewing produces a by-product unique to that method of extraction: crema. This is simply an emulsification of the fats in coffee as water is forced through the packed grounds at high pressure in combination with the outgassing of carbon dioxide that occurs in freshly roasted beans. Crema is regarded as an indication of quality, because the beans will emit carbon dioxide for only a short while after roasting, so it can point to how recently the beans have been roasted.

It should be noted that a number of other factors can affect the crema. Different varietals, growing locations and processing methods can alter the sugar and lipid content of a coffee bean, leading to a difference in the amount and type of crema produced, regardless of carbon dioxide levels.

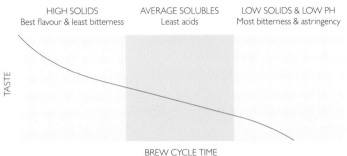

EXTRACTION OF SOLUBLE COMPOUNDS

HIGH SOLIDS	AVERAGE SOLUBLES	LOW SOLIDS & LOW PH
Best flavour & least bitterness	Least acids	Most bitterness & astringency

TASTE

BREW CYCLE TIME

contains much less water. Hence, the strength of the espresso is much higher than that of the regular coffee, because there is a higher ratio of TDS to water, though the percentage of available soluble materials extracted into the brew is much lower.

One common cause of strong yet underdeveloped coffee is using too much coffee for too short a brewing time, because the coffee materials that normally dissolve later in the extraction process have not had a chance to be released from the bean, and the high coffee-to-water ratio results in a higher proportion of first-stage soluble materials.

Conversely, you can also have weak and overdeveloped, or bitter, coffee. This results when the coffee-to-water ratio is not high enough to ensure an adequate percentage of coffee solubles, but a longer extraction time releases a high percentage of the solubles from the bean. In this case, 22 to 26 per cent of the solubles would have been released from the bean instead of the ideal of 20 per cent, taking the brew into bitter territory.

It will often require a lot of experimentation in modifying your brew to bring it within the optimum square on the brewing control chart, because there are many variables to take into consideration. Different brewing methods and/or environmental conditions can make consistency difficult to achieve, throwing off the balance of your cup even if those changes are only minor.

SOLUBLE FLAVOUR GROUPINGS

So what do these soluble materials mean for the process of extraction and the flavour of your coffee? Ted Lingle, former executive director of the Specialty Coffee Association of America (SCAA) as well as a coffee industry pioneer, was the first to group coffee flavours by molecular weight. These groupings assist in achieving balance in the cup by allowing analysis of the flavours to determine if the coffee is over- or underextracted. The four groups are as follows:

FRUITY ACIDS With floral and fruity aromas, these are some of the lightest flavour molecules and the first to become soluble during brewing.

MAILLARD COMPOUNDS Slightly slower to become soluble than the fruity acids, these are by-products of the roasting process that lend nutty, toasted grain or malty flavours.

BROWNING SUGAR/CARAMELS These impart sweet vanilla, chocolate or caramelized flavours. During the roasting process, most of the sugars are caramelized, the source of much of the coffee's sweetness. Highly caramelized sugars, such as those present in bittersweet dark roasts, take longer to extract.

DRY DISTILLATES Prominent in darker roasts, these are the especially dark caramels and Maillard compounds that lend ashy, smoky, carbon or tobacco flavours. These are the slowest to become soluble and can overwhelm many of the subtler flavours if present in high concentrations.

Going by taste alone and the four flavour groupings, extraction yield can be roughly gauged without the need for a refractometer or brew strength meter. If your coffee has overpowering characteristics of dry distillates or bitter caramels, it can be surmised that your brew is overextracted. Conversely, a brew that is too fruity or sour is probably underextracted. In either case, the balance of soluble materials is incorrect.

PROPORTION

Based on recommendations set out by the SCAA, the basic coffee-to-water ratio should be 10 grams (about 2 tablespoons) of ground coffee per 170 grams (¾ cup) of water. In practice, depending upon your brewing method and type of bean, you may only need as little as half that amount of coffee.

All coffee measurements are best made by weight instead of volume, because coffee beans are not consistent in size or density, and every scoop yields a marginally different amount. A good starting point is a coffee-to-water ratio of 1:17, or 10 grams (about 2 tablespoons) of coffee per 170 grams (¾ cup) of water, the size of a standard coffee cup. Although your espresso machine will often already be set to deliver a standard amount of water for a single or a double shot, the coffee grounds need to be measured accurately by weight in the portafilter to be sure of the correct ratio.

Experts differ in opinion as to the ideal weight of coffee grounds for an espresso shot, and the quantity required will vary according to your equipment and type of coffee beans. However, many people agree that, as a rough guide, 7 to 8 grams (about 1½ tablespoons) of coffee should be used for a single shot and 14 to 16 grams (about 3 tablespoons) of coffee for a double, depending on the size of your portafilter baskets. Many new speciality coffee bars and roasters consider this to be the traditional European style, and their dosages and methods differ from this approach substantially. Double shots are becoming the norm in most modern coffeehouses, with consumers now used to specifically requesting a single shot. Barista training is often carried out by small local roasters who operate in line with the principles of the Third Wave Coffee movement in recommending a dose of 18 to 20 grams (about ¼ cup) of coffee as standard for a double espresso shot.

These recommended coffee proportions should be used only as a guide. Using a digital kitchen scale (see page 110) will ensure you weigh the exact amount of coffee for your preferred strength and brew method.

WATER

Water is one of the most important components of a cup of coffee, because it makes up 98 to 99 per cent of your beverage. In all stages of the process, control over the amount, temperature and type of water is key to the quality of your coffee.

Distilled water should not be used for brewing coffee, because all minerals have been removed, and these are essential for taste and to aid the extraction process. It also has a relatively high acidity level of 5 to 6 pH, so it can actually be corrosive, causing damage to your equipment.

Hard water should also be avoided, because the minerals in it can block the plumbing of your coffee-maker by coating the pipes with chalky calcium deposits. Water that has been softened with tablets or by other means is also inadvisable, because the sodium ions used to soften the water can create a gelatinous mass that may clog up your machine.

WATER TYPES

Filtered water is the ideal choice for coffee making, because carafe, sink-based or charcoal filters remove chemicals and sediment while retaining important minerals. Bottled spring water is also suitable, but make sure that the mineral content is between 50 to 150 parts per million, because this level will give you the best-tasting water without being either too hard or too soft for coffee brewing. The maximum mineral content you should use in coffee brewing is 300 parts per million.

TEMPERATURE

Getting the temperature right is important because hot water dissolves the soluble solids present in the ground coffee, extracting the chemicals and constituents that give coffee its flavours and aromas. The ideal temperatures for brewing are between 91°C (196°F) and 96°C (205°F), and the closer to the higher figure, the better, although brewing coffee at the boiling point, or 100°C (212°F), can often result in bitterness. Water below a temperature of 91°C (196°F) will underextract, resulting in weak and tasteless coffee. Darker roasts are able to handle lower temperatures, making them an ideal option for inexpensive coffee machines that may have difficulty heating the water to the requisite temperature.

An easy way of approximating the correct water temperature is to take your kettle off the heat source for about thirty to sixty seconds after it reaches a boil, which will lower the temperature slightly to within the recommended range. Because the resting time required will differ depending on your type of kettle or the environmental temperature, another more precise method is to place a thermometer in your kettle and time how long it takes for the temperature to drop to within the required range.

PREWETTING

With filter and drip methods of brewing, you will need to prewet the coffee grounds with hot water. The moisture and heat allows the coffee to release carbon dioxide, preparing the coffee for extraction, and the grounds soak up a little of the water, swelling in size and beginning the brewing process. Although the degassing process – referred to as 'blooming', where the grounds foam up – is one that occurs naturally after roasting, the addition of hot water speeds up the process. It is also a good way of detecting how fresh your coffee is, because the less the coffee blooms, the more time has passed since roasting.

For instructions on how to prewet the coffee grounds and brew various types of coffee, refer to the instructions in section 6.

ACHIEVING BALANCE

So how does all this information on solubility, extraction, proportion and brewing water translate into a method of brewing guaranteed to deliver the ideal cup of coffee? The answer is it's all about balance: balance in flavour, balance in extraction and balance in measurement.

BALANCE IN FLAVOUR AND EXTRACTION

As we have seen earlier in this section, coffee flavours and aromatics become soluble at different stages of the coffee extraction process. Some soluble materials dissolve soon after the addition of water and heat, and others take longer to break down. A perfect demonstration of this is to set up an espresso shot, weighing and timing it to achieve a good extraction, and then prepare another shot and divide the resulting extraction into thirds. For example, if your shot was perfectly extracted at twenty-seven seconds, split the second extraction into three cups of nine seconds' extraction each. Your first cup – the first third of the extraction – will be strong, oily, acidic and sour; the second cup – the second third of the extraction – will be full of the sugars and caramels; and the final third will be weak and bitter.

If you prefer less bitterness, try shutting off your shot midway into the last third; if you prefer more bitterness, let the shot run longer. As long as you have started with a correct extraction, you can now use this split-shot trial to determine the balance of your flavours.

The extraction process itself also requires balance among the various factors involved – temperature, extraction yield, time and TDS – with each needing to be within its optimal range.

BALANCE IN MEASUREMENT

Just as in baking, a difference of a few grams when measuring coffee grounds or water can completely throw off the balance of your cup. When making espresso, the difference of even a single gram can lead to your cup being over- or underextracted, so even the best-calibrated machine will not be able to guarantee consistency in your shots. However, if the coffee grounds are accurately measured, if the grind remains at a uniform level, and if there are not too many fluctuations in the immediate environment, you should be able to extract consistent espresso shots time after time.

The same goes for regular coffee – if you determine the ratio of water and coffee grounds that suits your personal preference, weighing your grounds will ensure a consistent, balanced cup each and every time.

ESPRESSO TASTE

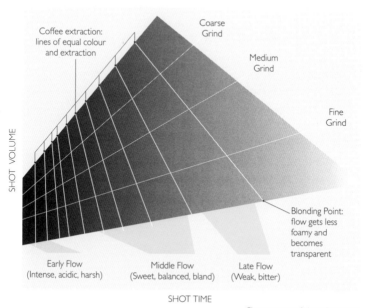

Coffee extraction: lines of equal colour and extraction

Coarse Grind

Medium Grind

Fine Grind

SHOT VOLUME

Blonding Point: flow gets less foamy and becomes transparent

Early Flow
(Intense, acidic, harsh)

Middle Flow
(Sweet, balanced, bland)

Late Flow
(Weak, bitter)

SHOT TIME

Chart courtesty of Home-Barista.com

AROMA AND FLAVOUR

As a beverage, coffee can be consumed on its own and appreciated on its own merits, or it can be enjoyed with or after a meal. However, there are various ways of matching coffee with food to bring out the distinct flavours of the brew and, indeed, vice versa.

Coffee is commonly considered of secondary importance when consumed with food – an after-dinner beverage and almost an afterthought. However, the tables can sometimes be turned and food can be seen as a means of enhancing appreciation of coffee. In Italy, for example, coffee is often served with a small cookie to nibble in between sips. In this way, the sweetness does not mask the coffee flavours, because it is not added to the beverage, and the coffee remains pure and unadulterated. Any additional sweetness comes from sugar lingering from the cookie, pronouncing the flavours of the coffee instead of drowning them.

Traditional cookies or cakes are not the only foods that can bring out the flavours in coffee. Pairing coffee with a cereal bar, for example, can accentuate the beverage's nutty, fruity flavours, while the bitter strength of dark, strong brews can be balanced by the sweetness of dried fruits or bittersweet chocolate. Coffee, in this way, is comparable to wine. Its aroma, flavour, mouthfeel and acidity can be evaluated and matched to various foods, using a science-based process designed to highlight the nuanced flavours of each bean.

FOOD PAIRINGS

Food chemists and scientists have researched food pairings extensively, and have found that food and drink with similar flavours or aroma compounds combine well together. Coffee, again like wine, is often described as having notes of berry, chocolate, fruit or citrus, and these dominant flavours can be used to match corresponding flavours in foods. For example, coffees with a full body and spiced, chocolate or nutty notes combine well with creamy, sweet desserts or good-quality chocolate; semi-washed (see page 30) and dry or natural processed coffees (see page 27) heavy with notes of stone fruit, berries and overlying sweetness pair well with light pastries and fruits; aromatic citrus-scented coffees match well with dried apricots and orange or lemon cakes; and warm, vanilla-scented coffees go well with rice puddings, honey, caramel or waffles and pancakes. Remember, however, that the coffee flavours can vary according to the brewing method, and this is another way to accentuate various aspects of your brew.

Just as food has the potential to complement and enhance a good cup of coffee, you'll find that coffee can do the same for food. The best way to begin experimenting with pairing is to match flavour to flavour – notes of chocolate to chocolate; berry notes to raspberries. You can then branch out from there, drawing on successful food combinations. For example, raspberry, chocolate and mint are a delightful combination in food, so coffee with hints of berry would pair nicely with a chocolate mint cookie.

If you use this simple approach, you will find it easy to pair food and coffee successfully. The most important thing is to develop your ability to analyse flavour and aroma. The flavour wheel shown on pages 94–95 will be a useful tool in helping you build your skills of descriptive analysis.

TASTER'S FLAVOUR WHEEL

BODY

Light	Watery
	Tea-like
	Silky
	Slick
	Juicy
Medium	Smooth
	2% Milk
	Syrupy
	Round
	Creamy
Heavy	Full
	Velvety
	Big
	Chewy
	Coating

FLORAL
- Lemongrass
- Orange Blossom
- Jasmine Honeysuckle
- Magnolia
- Lavender
- Rose Hips
- Hibiscus
- Bergamot
- Hops
- Black Tea
- Green Tea
- Mint
- Sage
- Dill

VEGETAL
- Grassy
- Mangetout
- Sweet Pea
- Squash
- Mushroom
- Green Pepper
- Olive
- Leafy Greens
- Hay/Straw

EARTHY
- Tobacco
- Cedar
- Fresh Wood
- Soil

HERB

SAVOURY
- Tomato
- Sundried Tomato
- Soy Sauce
- Meat-Like
- Leathery

SPICE
- Clove
- Licorice-Anise
- Curry
- Nutmeg
- Ginger
- Coriander
- Cinnamon
- White Pepper
- Black Pepper

ROAST
- Carbon
- Smokey
- Burnt Sugar
- Toast

GRAIN & CEREAL
- Fresh Bread
- Barley
- Wheat
- Rye
- Digestive Biscuit
- Granola
- Sweet Bread Pastry

NUT
- Almond
- Hazelnut
- Pecan
- Cashew
- Peanut
- Walnut

The coffee taster's flavour wheel helps identify flavours and tastes present in coffee. Using this wheel to help you identify flavours, you can describe your cup with greater accuracy, and also identify what foods will pair well with your brew.

ADJECTIVES & INTENSIFIERS FOR COFFEEE

Crisp, bright, vibrant, tart	Muted, dull, mild
Wild, unbalanced, sharp, pointed	Structured, balanced, rounded
Dense, deep, complex	Soft, faint, delicate
Juicy	Dry, astringent
Lingering, dirty	Quick, clean

CITRUS — Lemon & Lemonade, Lime, Grapefruit, Clementine, Tangerine, Mandarin Orange, Orange

APPLE/PEAR — Green Apple, Red Apple

MELON — Watermelon, Honeydew, Cantaloupe

GRAPE — White Grape, Green Grape, Red Grape, Black Grape

TROPICAL FRUIT — Lychee, Star Fruit, Tamarind, Passion Fruit, Pineapple, Mango, Papaya, Kiwi, Banana, Coconut

STONE FRUIT — Peach, Nectarine, Apricot, Plum, Cherry, Black Cherry

BERRY — Cranberry, Raspberry, Strawberry, Blueberry, Redcurrant, Blackcurrant

DRIED FRUIT — Golden Raisin, Raisin, Dried Fig, Dried Dates, Prunes

FRUIT

CHOCOLATE — Cacao Nibs, Dark Chocolate, Baker's Chocolate, Bittersweet Chocolate, Cocoa Powder, Milk Chocolate

SWEET & SUGARY — Vanilla, Nougat, Honey, Butter, Cream, Marshmallow, Sugar Cane, Brown Sugar, Caramel, Maple Syrup, Molasses, Cola

Graphic courtesy of Counter Culture Coffee

Coffee & Technology

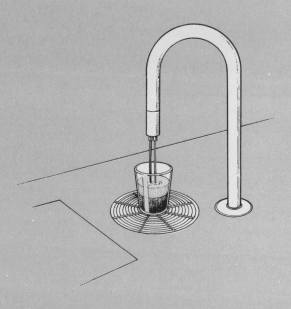

SIMPLE COFFEEPOT

There are a number of different ways to brew coffee without the use of gadgets or machines. One such method is cowboy coffee, which is made simply by boiling water with coffee grounds in a pot set over a campfire, known as decoction (see page 120).

Turkish or Greek coffee also employs the decoction method and is one of the oldest ways of brewing coffee still in use today. Although simple to make and requiring few utensils, the quality of the equipment determines that of the end product. The coffee grind needed for this coffee is especially fine, generally obtainable from only a high-quality coffee grinder, because most domestic grinding appliances cannot grind to a sufficiently fine powder. An affordable option is to purchase a special Turkish coffee grinder to provide the appropriate fineness.

This type of coffee also involves the use of a special pot for brewing, called a *cezve* in Turkey, or *briki* in Greece, but usually termed *ibrik* in the West. Its hourglass shape is important in several ways. It enables the coffee to be poured easily, because it provides a funnel up the neck and out through the spout. The shape of the neck also allows for the liquid to be poured out while retaining the bulk of the coffee grounds in the pot. Most important, the narrowed neck is crucial for developing foam, essential to the brewing process of Turkish coffee. The aim is to heat the coffee until it reaches the foaming stage but to keep it at that point by lifting the pot off and then placing it back onto the heat source (see page 122).

Ibrik

SIPHON/VACUUM

The somewhat labour-intensive siphon/vacuum method of brewing is well-known for producing an especially clear, not cloudy, cup. The siphon/vacuum coffee-maker was invented in the early 1800s but lost popularity in the 1900s. However, it has recently attracted renewed interest from coffee connoisseurs, who are interested in bringing the focus back to quality instead of concentrating on convenience.

This coffee-maker operates on the principle of the expansion and contraction of water vapour. It comprises two glass vessels, attached by a siphon that allows water to pass between them, and it is suspended over a heating source. The water is placed in the bottom, and a rubber seal creates a partial vacuum in the lower vessel. Once the coffee-maker is placed over a heat source, the vapour from the water expands on heating and the pressure from the vapour pushes the hot water up the siphon into the top vessel, where the coffee grounds are added, stirred and then steeped. Once brewing has finished, the heat source is turned off. Upon cooling, the water vapour contracts and the pressure in the lower vessel consequently drops. A partial vacuum of negative pressure is created, sucking the liquid back down through the siphon to fill the lower vessel with the brewed coffee.

Other vacuum-based brewing methods include the Clover machine, a recently invented high-tech brewing system that can now be found in speciality coffee bars worldwide. This single-cup brewer takes up a comparatively large amount of counter real estate. The barista places the ground coffee over a fine filter that sits atop a piston, which then descends into the machine. After the coffee has been steeped, the piston pushes back up, creating a vacuum and sucking the brewed coffee down through valves. The piston then descends once more, pushing the brewed coffee out of the bottom of the machine into the cup waiting below. The filter rises until it is flush with the top of the machine, and the spent grounds, now sitting in a puck, are then scraped off. The Clover is acknowledged for producing clear, crisp coffee that highlights the nuanced flavours of the varietal or region.

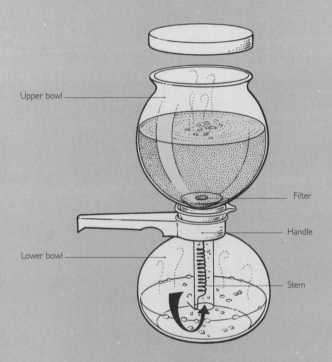

Upper bowl

Filter

Handle

Lower bowl

Stem

THE MACCHINETTA

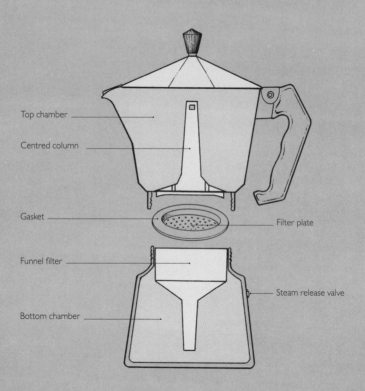

Top chamber

Centred column

Gasket

Funnel filter

Bottom chamber

Filter plate

Steam release valve

STEAM POWER

Coffee is one of the most widely consumed beverages in the world, and people are constantly devising new ways – or reinventing old ways – to brew and consume this popular drink.

Before the advent of espresso, it took up to five laborious minutes to brew a cup of coffee. To make the process faster, easier and more effective, new techniques were frequently developed. Inventors and scientists across Europe saw a money-making opportunity in the enduring popularity of coffee. Vast numbers of coffee machines were designed in the nineteenth century, many of which used steam power.

While various people contributed to the creation of the espresso machine, the first-known patent was registered by a Turin café owner, Angelo Moriondo, in the late 1800s. Unfortunately, he limited use of the machine to his own cafés, so it was never mass-produced. In 1901, another Italian, Luigi Bezzera, patented a design, although he was unable to produce and market it until Desiderio Pavoni provided financial backing to make his invention commercially viable. Bezzeras were perhaps the first espresso machines, but essentially they were huge boilers with outputs on either side. A major problem was the amount of steam that came into direct contact with the coffee beans. The direct heat caused bitterness and off-flavours in the cup, and the steam pressure was not high enough to extract adequately.

A few steam-powered machines for making strong black coffee are still used in homes today. While not producing what we know as espresso, the macchinetta, or moka or espresso pot, relies on the same basic extraction method as the early espresso machines. It is a stovetop kettle, similar in principle to a percolator (see page 104). However, instead of hot water making its way up the inner tube and then falling back to mix with the water that has not yet passed through the coffee grounds, the macchinetta uses a mixture of steam and pressure to push the water from the lower chamber, through the coffee grounds, to the upper chamber where the brewed coffee is separated, ready to be consumed.

THE GAGGIA

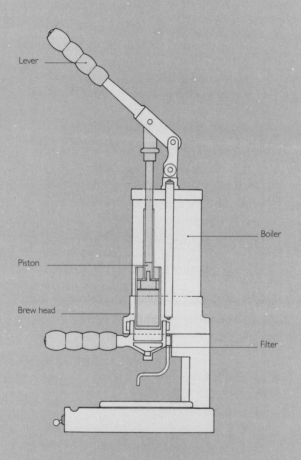

Lever

Piston

Brew head

Boiler

Filter

PISTON POWER

Although the steam-powered coffee machine was capable of producing a decent cup of coffee, it simply could not provide enough pressure to extract a satisfactory espresso shot.

The challenge to find ways to increase the pressure using, variously, pumps, hydraulics and pistons, culminated in the manufacture of the first truly viable solution – a machine designed by Achille Gaggia in 1938 that used hand-powered pistons. Some European-style coffee bars and aficionados continue to use hand-powered piston machines, claiming that manual operation allows for greater control over the shot. These impressive machines can certainly make flavourful espresso, but they also demand a high level of skill, because many elements need to be managed to ensure correct compression of the lever and extraction of the shot.

The Gaggia revolutionized coffee making by creating espresso as we know it today. It still uses steam, but the steam is never directly in contact with the coffee. Instead, steam creates pressure in the boiler, forcing the water into a cylinder where it is further pressurized by the pistons. The original manual operation produced the phrase 'pulling a shot', because baristas needed to pull the pistons up and down; most machines now use electricity.

Achille Gaggia not only changed the flavour and brewing method of what was already one of the world's most popular food products, but he also discovered an aspect of coffee that now is considered of great importance – *crema*. The first espresso consumers called this layer of coffee oils 'scum', because it was seen as an unwanted by-product of the high-pressure coffee extraction method. Gaggia needed a marketing campaign to push his new product, so he installed his coffee machines in bars around Milan along with a sign that read *caffè crema di caffè natural* (coffee cream from natural coffee). Once consumers recognized that the coffee extracted by these machines was of a superior quality, high-end bars and restaurants started to install Gaggia machines, and eventually this style of coffee making spread beyond Milan – and from there gradually took over the world.

ELECTRICAL POWER

Electricity was an immensely important factor in the evolution of coffee, radically changing the way coffee was prepared and consumed. With it came automation and consistency, and this enabled consumers to brew coffee at home that was closer to what they could order in a café.

PERCOLATORS

The invention of the electric coffee percolator was one of the first meetings between electricity and coffee. Offering a basic way to brew, the electric percolator was at first regarded as a high-value kitchen item, because it brewed coffee quicker and was much more convenient than the stovetop method. Before long it became a commonplace, if not essential, kitchen appliance and was relegated far from the realm of luxury. Many coffee consumers now recommend drip or automatic coffee-makers over percolators, but nevertheless there are a significant number of people who continue to enjoy percolated coffee.

Percolation is not the most well-regarded method of coffee extraction for many people for the following reasons. It sends the water through the coffee grounds multiple times, and the coffee sometimes boils during the process of extracting the entire batch. The water temperature is also often retained at a higher level than in many other coffee extraction methods, adding to bitterness and potentially resulting in overextraction. Those who prefer stronger, darker, more bitter brews may find percolated coffee a suitable choice for a quick morning brew. A popular method up to the 1970s, the percolator has since been largely replaced by the drip coffee machine (see page 106), which is generally believed to make a better-quality brew.

The matter of selecting the best coffee beans for percolating comes down to personal preference, but, in any event, the grind should be coarse. This means that less surface area of the coffee comes into contact with the water, allowing time for the flavour components to be extracted and reducing bitterness.

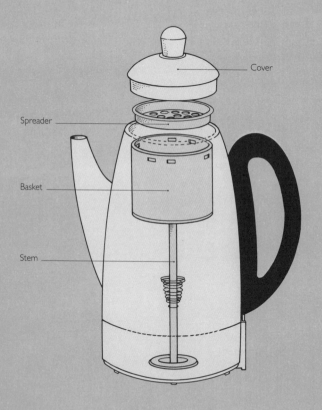

Cover

Spreader

Basket

Stem

AUTOMATIC DRIP COFFEE

While drip coffee has long been a popular way of brewing coffee manually, it did not become popular in North America until the invention of electrically powered, automatic drip coffee-makers. Valued for their convenience, the one downside of these coffee-makers is the lack of control a consumer has over the extraction. The machine itself largely determines time and temperature, so it is important to purchase a good-quality, well-calibrated machine produced by a respected manufacturer.

Electrically powered coffee-makers became popular for several reasons. Safe heating elements negated the need to use an oven, and the invention of the automatic cut-off switch was revolutionary. Previously, coffee brewing required an active participant to keep a watchful eye on the temperature, time and extraction level at all times. Suddenly the task could be largely turned over to a machine. Most types of manually operated coffee brewers were adapted for electrical power, either by simply adding a heating element to the bottom of a coffeepot or automating the entire process.

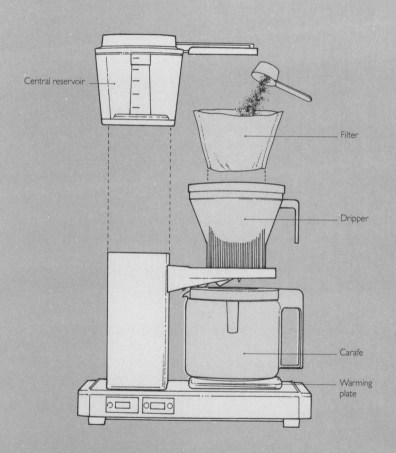

Central reservoir

Filter

Dripper

Carafe

Warming plate

CONVENIENCE MACHINES

Aimed at the convenience crowd, dozens of new coffee machines claim to produce a café-quality beverage at the push of a button. Pod-type coffee machines create café-style espresso beverages by extracting an 'espresso' shot from individual pods filled with a measured dose of coffee. Milk can often also be put into the machine to be frothed while the coffee brews; the consumer needs only to pour one into the other.

There are also equally smart machines that brew specific beverages, such as café latte. Typically, they consist of a drip-style pitcher to hold the milk and an upper compartment that holds the coffee grounds and water. The machine then froths the milk and extracts the coffee into the pitcher – a latte at the touch of a button. Then there are high-end espresso machines, designed to replicate the steps a competent barista would take to brew a good cup of coffee and ensure consistency by repeating them with mechanical precision time after time.

Various cupping tests of these machines are largely inconclusive. Some produce coffee that ranks only slightly higher than instant; others are embraced by Michelin-starred restaurants, producing coffee that experts deem to be top quality. Debates ensue on whether mechanization has devalued an art form, but many people appreciate the convenience and ease with which coffee can now be brewed.

Good coffee is subjective – if you enjoy the taste of coffee brewed from a single-cup machine or a café latte maker, then the machine has done its job. However, it is perfectly possible to spend a small fortune on these new-generation coffee-makers designed for coffee lovers in a hurry. But are these machines able to match the aroma, mouthfeel and flavour of freshly brewed coffee made by a more old-fashioned brewing method? Using premium beans and state-of-the-art equipment does not in itself ensure an excellent cup of coffee. It also takes knowledge and skill in measuring, tamping, grinding and extracting to make a great tasting cup of coffee.

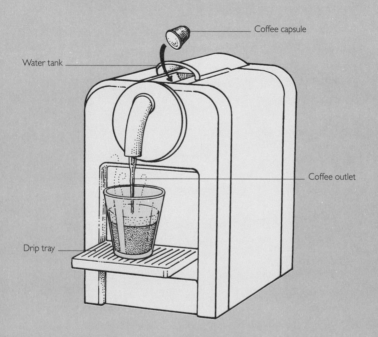

Coffee capsule

Water tank

Coffee outlet

Drip tray

GADGETS

Some people prefer minimalist coffee-making methods, using only a pot, flame, coffee grounds and water to create their perfect brew, whereas others are enthusiastic about using an array of nifty gadgets to help them brew the ideal cup of coffee.

Coffee-making appliances and machines are covered elsewhere in the book (see section 6), but this section focuses on all those milk frothers, tampers, mats and thermometers that coffee aficionados can invest in to build a collection of special equipment for tweaking a brew to their individual specifications.

DIGITAL KITCHEN SCALE

Most home cooks and home baristas measure ingredients by volume, but the most accurate way to measure coffee – or any ingredient for that matter – is by weight. An accurate digital kitchen scale should, therefore, be a part of every coffee lover's collection of equipment, and everyone should be familiar with how to measure the perfect quantity of coffee. While coffee consumers will go to great lengths to source superior beans, test many different brewing methods, and research and purchase various (and often expensive) items of coffee-making equipment, the accurate measurement of their grounds is often the last thing they consider, and the predominant measure of coffee is the scoop, which is not precise enough to ensure consistency.

There are huge variations in the size and weight of different beans, which means that measuring them by volume will yield varying weights. The taste of your cup can be discernibly altered by even a 1- to 2-gram difference in weight, so it is vital to ensure consistency.

A number of different types of scale are available, from expensive, speciality coffee scales that have built-in timers and measure weight, time and flow rates, to inexpensive, battery-powered digital kitchen scales. If money is no object, the former will give you exact readings so that you can be sure of consistency every time. These scales can detect weight changes down to 0.1 of a gram, detecting evapouration and calculating flow rate, and some can even sync with your mobile phone to allow you to record your brewing process.

Scales of this calibre are not necessary to brew a perfect cup. Although the aforementioned features are interesting and allow for fine tweaking of your brewing method, all you really need is a digital kitchen scale that is accurate down to 0.1 of a gram and has a 'tare' function, whereby the weight of the weighing container can be automatically subtracted, resetting the scale to zero. This type of scale is available online and in some larger department stores.

TAMPER AND MAT

Required for espresso and home espresso machines, a good tamper lets you press the coffee grounds into your portafilter with enough pressure to provide a bed of resistance for the hot water – the tamper also smoothes the surface of the coffee and ensures even distribution of the grounds. A mat provides a slightly spongy surface for ease in pressing down and protects the counter from marks from the portafilter or coffee grounds.

When buying a tamper, there are several things to look for. Choose a tamper that is relatively weighty, because it will make it easier to compress the grounds. The handle should fit your hand well and not be uncomfortable to push down. Ideally, tampers should be made from metal; plastic tampers often fail to compress the grounds sufficiently and are uncomfortable to use. The most important factor is the size of the tamper: make sure it is the exact size of your portafilter.

THERMOMETER

This is another kitchen must-have that can help you perfect your cup of coffee. Mainly used to avoid burning or scalding milk as you heat and froth it, it is also useful for testing water temperature to ensure that your equipment is performing accurately.

MILK FROTHERS

While many espresso machines will have a steam wand attached for the specific purpose of frothing milk, other types of coffee-makers do not incorporate a milk frother, and many people who brew their coffee using other methods may still want to replicate the frothy milk typical of lattes or cappuccinos. The most common varieties of milk frothers are detailed below.

HANDPRESS MILK FROTHER This is similar to a French press in design, where you pump the press up and down, in this case creating air bubbles in the milk and, thus, causing it to froth. It does not have a heating element, so the milk has to be heated prior to frothing. It is labour-intensive to operate and may fail to texture the milk adequately, but it is inexpensive and can create frothy milk fairly quickly.

HAND-HELD MILK FROTHER This small, inexpensive frother works in the same way as a hand-held miniature electric mixer, and if sufficiently good in quality, it can make fairly acceptable frothed milk, although the texture of the milk may be lacking.

ELECTRIC MILK FROTHER You simply pour your milk into this tube-shaped appliance and replace the lid, and the gadget then warms and steams your milk, frothing it to the required consistency and temperature. This type of frother generally consists of an electric base for warming the milk and stainless steel beaters inside.

OVENTOP MILK STEAMER A oventop version of the steam wand attached to an espresso machine, this gadget heats up water in a kettle and emits steam from a wand extending from the kettle body. This type of frother is often slow at the task and can also be dangerous to operate; you must constantly keep an eye on the pressure valve so that it does not exceed the maximum. Follow the manufacturer's directions, because individual models differ. Although expensive, it does offer the capacity to make espresso machine–quality frothed milk at home.

MILK FROTHERS

Handpress milk frother

Hand-held milk frother

Electric milk frother

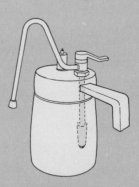

Oventop milk steamer

CHOICE OF CUP

Throughout history, coffee has been consumed from hundreds of different varieties of vessel in countless shapes, sizes and materials. Many cultures have a traditional way of serving and consuming coffee. But does the form this paraphernalia takes really affect the taste of the final brew?

CERAMIC MUGS AND CUPS

The generic mug has been a staple of Western culture for hundreds of years. The most conventional and sturdy form of drinking vessel, the mug was used for alcoholic, medicinal and other varieties of beverage long before coffee was widely consumed. The shape and size is designed to hold a large quantity of the beverage of choice and in early times was carved out of wood or made of hand-formed pottery.

Now mainly crafted from porcelain, bone china, earthenware and other ceramics, the coffee mug is ubiquitous in many kitchens worldwide. Why is it so popular? Maybe it's the fact that you can purchase mugs in any size, colour or design you like. Or perhaps it's because it is one of the most practical methods of delivery – fill up your mug once and you are supplied with an ample serving. However, the main benefit of a ceramic mug lies in its insulating properties – the thick walls of the mug are designed to retain heat for a longer period than mugs made from other materials.

DISPOSABLE CUPS

In the modern world, a large percentage of coffee is consumed from disposable paper, plastic or foam cups. Porous and sometimes containing chemical compounds that may pose a risk to human health, such as bisphenol A (BPA), these are the least recommended receptacles in which to serve coffee. Foam and plastic will often retain heat for longer than paper cups, but the beverage and the heat can erode the cups, potentially leaching the chemicals they contain into your coffee.

Paper cups lose heat fast, and life-cycle assessments of these products indicate that they can have a much larger impact on the environment than ceramic or glass cups, taking into consideration washing, transport, disposal and production costs.[1] Many people agree that the taste of coffee is altered when it is served in foam or plastic, whereas others say they prefer the taste of coffee served in paper to ceramic. Ultimately, it is a matter of personal preference.

REUSABLE TAKEAWAY CUPS

A trend in recent years in response to public awareness of environmental issues is the moulded, reusable takeaway cup. A replica of the conventional paper or plastic takeaway coffee cup, it is designed to hold a regular-size coffee but can be washed and reused. Generally constructed from a BPA-free plastic, these higher-quality cups are designed to last for more than five hundred uses. Brands such as KeepCup make barista-standard reusable cups available in standard coffee cup sizes and shaped to allow ease of use with espresso machines.

OTHER CUPS

The demitasse is a small cup, usually made from the same ceramic material as a generic coffee cup or mug, used to serve espresso and Turkish coffee. Translating from the French literally as 'half cup', it is generally about ¼ cup to ⅓ cup (around 2 to 3 fl oz) in capacity.

Less popular than ceramic, glass coffee cups are used for a variety of coffee beverages. In Australia and some other countries, café lattes are served in a mid-height glass, some resembling a water glass, while other coffee mugs or glasses have a stemmed base and are fitted with a handle, such as those used for the alcoholic Irish coffee.

[1] Refiller, Bern. 2013. 'Lifecycle Assessment: reusable mugs versus disposable cups.' http://www.refiller.ch/download/pictures/8e/6r4go51v89r9avzdf7ob0yvkolr4sv/refiller_coffee_comparison.pdf

Metal was one of the original materials used for crafting drinking vessels for hot drinks and is still used today. However, metal cups can be difficult to hold, because metal conducts heat. Traditional Turkish coffee cups were sometimes made from metal, and although most are now porcelain, often painted or decorated with foil, some are still made in the traditional way from metals such as copper, often with fine details and designs.

THERMOSES AND CARAFES

Throughout history, people have devised various methods to ensure that hot drinks retain their heat, from leaving a pot over a heat source – which can often lead to overextraction in the case of coffee – to selecting heat-retentive materials from which to fashion drinking vessels. However, the real breakthrough came with the invention of the vacuum flask, or thermos. It comprises two flasks, a smaller one inside a larger one, with a space between them that acts as a vacuum, preventing heat transfer and loss. This enables coffee, or any other hot liquid, to be stored and kept hot for an extended period. Thermal carafes work in much the same way, although sometimes they are simply made from a thick insulating material. Carafes are, however, intended primarily for serving, while the main purpose of a thermos is to transport a hot beverage.

COFFEE CUPS

Turkish cup

Irish cup

Demitasse

How to Make Coffee

MAKING COFFEE

Now that you have explored the science behind brewing coffee, this chapter provides step-by-step guides to putting that knowledge into practice to make the perfect cup using each of the main brewing methods.

The preceding sections of this book have covered the diverse nature of coffee and explained the various factors that can influence its character and flavour, including the type of bean and growing region, roast level and grind, and brewing method and temperature. Added to that, there are also many ways in which you can prepare and serve coffee, which differ according to culture and the equipment used. And that is even before you bring personal preference into the picture – brewed weak or strong, or bitter, sweet, fruity or floral; served with cold or hot milk, flat or frothed; sweetened with sugar or spiced with cardamom or cinnamon.

Measuring out ingredients by weight is the most accurate way of getting the perfect cup of coffee, so if you can, pick up a digital kitchen scale with metric measurements (measuring in grams is more precise than in ounces) from a kitchen speciality store or the kitchen section in some larger department stores. Look for one with a 'tare' button, which subtracts the weight of the bowl or other container (and any contents), so you know precisely how much the ingredient being added weighs. These recipes are only a starting point, enabling you to adjust and modify the approach to suit your own requirements.

COWBOY COFFEE

This is one of the easiest ways of brewing coffee, using the decoction method of extraction, where water is boiled with the coffee grounds in a pot for a few minutes to make a crude brew. It is ideally suited to camping or backpacking, because a small grinder is compact enough to carry with you and there is no need to measure the coffee accurately. In the worst-case scenario, you can buy freshly roasted beans and coarsely grind them before you leave home.

YOU WILL NEED
Small burr grinder, measuring spoon, large mug, pot, heat source, timer, coffee cups, water, freshly roasted coffee beans

METHOD

1 Grind your coffee beans coarsely using the burr grinder.

2 Measure out 220 grams of ground coffee per large mug of cold water (2 tablespoons/just under 1 cup). Pour the measured water into the pot.

3 Bring the water to a boil over a heat source. Remove and let stand for 30 to 60 seconds to lower the temperature slightly.

4 Add the coffee to the hot water, stirring to wet the grounds.

5 Let the pot stand for 2 minutes, then stir again and let stand for another 2 minutes. Cover the pot to retain the heat.

6 The grounds should have sunk to the bottom of the pot, so without disturbing the water too much, carefully pour the coffee into cups. If any grounds transfer, let the coffee sit in the cups for 30 seconds or so to let them settle to the bottom.

COWBOY COFFEE METHOD

STEP 2

STEP 3

STEP 4

STEP 6

TURKISH COFFEE

This traditional method of brewing coffee using decoction produces a rich, dark, strong cup. Domestic blade and burr grinders are rarely able to grind the coffee finely enough, but if you are unable to find a speciality Turkish grinder, grind the coffee as finely as your grinder can manage.

YOU WILL NEED

Ibrik (Turkish coffeepot), digital scale with metric readings, Turkish coffee cup, heat source, spoon, Turkish hand coffee grinder, water, freshly roasted coffee beans, sugar (optional)

METHOD

1 Place the coffeepot on the scale and tare or set to zero. Measure out the water you need by filling your Turkish coffee cup with cold water and then pour it into the pot. The water should just reach the neck of the pot so, if necessary, add more water to make a little extra coffee, but make sure that the water does not rise above the water line marked on the inside of your pot. Make note of the total weight of the water.

2 Place the pot on the heat source and heat the water until warm.

3 Measure out your coffee, using slightly more than with a French press (see page 144) – start with a ratio of 8 grams (about 5 teaspoons) of coffee per 100 grams (scant ½ cup) of water. Adjust to more or less coffee if you like your drink stronger or weaker, but note that the Turkish coffee method produces a relatively strong brew.

4 Grind the coffee to a fine powder using the Turkish hand grinder.

5 Place your coffee grounds on top of the water but do not stir them in. If you are adding sugar, add it on top now.

TURKISH COFFEE METHOD

STEP 1

STEP 5

STEP 7

STEP 8

6 Heat the pot over low heat, and after a few minutes you will notice the coffee foaming up the neck of the pot. Take hold of the handle and remove the pot from the heat source, letting the foam subside.

7 Once the foam has subsided, repeat step 6. You can then repeat one or two times, or stop at this point; try your coffee at different stages of the process to determine your preference. If you like, you can stir the coffee each time it subsides; again, you can try your coffee both ways and compare the results.

8 Most of the coffee will have fallen to the bottom of the pot at this stage. Distribute the coffee evenly by pouring a little into each cup in turn and then returning to the first cup and repeating until each is filled.

9 Wait for a few minutes for the foam and coffee to settle before you drink.

DRIP OR FILTER COFFEE

There are a number of drip or filter coffee-making methods, some producing a better-quality cup than others. Using the ubiquitous automatic drip coffee-maker is one of the most popular ways of brewing coffee in the United States, and it is an easy option for the home. Other methods, such as the pour-over, single-cup drip filter, are sold at high prices at speciality coffee bars.

'For all drip/filter coffee methods, use 60 to 65 grams of coffee for every litre [kilogram] of water – scale as required. If your cup is too weak, grassy or sour, use a finer grind. If your cup is too strong or bitter, user a coarser grind.'

MATTHEW PERGER
WORLD CHAMPION BARISTA, ST ALI AND SENSORY LAB, AUSTRALIA

Automatic Drip Coffee-maker

While not the most consistent or high-quality method of brewing, using an automatic drip coffee-maker is a no-fuss way of making coffee that does not require much attention. However, there are a few ways to make sure that you get the best cup you can from the machine.

YOU WILL NEED

Automatic drip coffee-maker, paper filter (if required), kettle, digital kitchen scale, burr grinder, spoon, coffee cups, water, freshly roasted coffee beans

METHOD

1 Set the drip coffee-maker up following the manufacturer's directions. If using a paper filter, boil some water, pour it over the installed filter and then empty the water out – this will rinse away some of the paper flavour that can transfer to your cup.

AUTOMATIC DRIP COFFEE METHOD

STEP 2

STEP 3

STEP 4

STEP 6

2 Pour water into the brewing reservoir following the manufacturer's directions.

3 Measure the coffee beans out according to how much water you are using: 60 to 65 grams per 1 kilogram (or litre) water (see panel below), adjusting to personal preference if a weaker or stronger brew is desired. Use the burr grinder to grind the coffee beans to medium and place in the filter.

4 Start the coffee-maker.

5 As soon as the coffee-maker has completed the brewing process, remove the coffee from the heat source – leaving it on the heat can make it bitter and negatively affect the taste.

6 Serve immediately, or keep in the carafe off the heat for up to 10 minutes.

MEASURING WATER

Water measures equally in millilitres or grams – for example, 100 millilitres of water equals 100 grams of water (which is 1 tablespoon short of ½ cup). Because you will already be measuring your coffee beans by weight, it is easier to measure water by weight, too. As with other brewing methods, 60 to 65 grams (about ¾ cup) of coffee beans should be used per 1 kilogram (about 4⅓ cups) of water, so the quantities of coffee beans and water for a typical cup of coffee would be 14 to 15 grams (about 3 tablespoons) of coffee beans and 240 grams (1 cup) of water.

Pour-over

Manual single-cup drip filters come in various shapes and sizes. A paper filter sits inside a conical dripper with an opening at the bottom. Boiling water is poured over the coffee and drips through into a receptacle placed below. This method of drip coffee produces a much better cup than an automatic drip coffee-maker, because the exact water temperature and brewing time can be manually controlled.

YOU WILL NEED
Paper filter to fit the shape and size of the filter cone, pour-over drip filter cone, receptacle, kettle, digital kitchen scale, burr grinder, spoon, coffee cup, water, freshly roasted coffee beans

METHOD

1 Put a paper filter into the filter cone and place the cone on your receptacle. Bring some water to a boil in the kettle. Before adding the coffee, pour hot water over the entire paper filter to rinse it through. Discard this water before starting to brew.

2 Measure the coffee beans out (see page 127). and use the grinder to grind them medium-fine. Deposit the ground coffee in the filter.

3 Set the filter cone, paper filter and receptacle on the scale, then tare or set the scale to zero.

4 Wet all the coffee grounds with hot water from the kettle, starting in the middle and pouring around in concentric circles. Pour only enough to saturate the grounds and let it 'bloom', or foam up (see page 89), for 30 seconds.

5 Continue to pour water evenly in circles outwards to the edge of the filter until you have reached the correct weight of water to coffee grounds (see page 127).

6 The water should take a few minutes to filter through, and once it slows to a drip, your clear, crisp brew will be ready to serve.

POUR-OVER METHOD

STEP 1

STEP 3

STEP 4

STEP 6

PERCOLATOR

Coffee percolators have largely been replaced by drip filters, but many people still use them to brew a simple cup of coffee at home – and they are also popular for an easy brew while camping or hiking. Electric or oventop, they work by spraying hot water over ground coffee beans, with the extracted coffee then collecting in the bottom of the percolator, ready to serve.

YOU WILL NEED

Coffee percolator, digital kitchen scale, burr grinder, water, freshly roasted coffee beans

METHOD

1 Place the coffee stem into the bottom of the percolator.

2 Fill the bottom reservoir with water up to just below the line on the stem where the filter basket will sit.

3 Place the filter basket onto the stem.

4 Measure 15 grams (just under ¼ cup) coffee beans per cup and use the burr grinder to grind them coarsely. Transfer the ground coffee to the filter basket.

5 Place the lid on the percolator.

6 Place the percolator on the heat source and heat the water (if you are using an electric percolator, turn it on).

7 Wait for the water to boil and start brewing. The percolator will start to 'perk' (make a spurting sound). When this sound starts to die down, your coffee is ready.

8 Serve immediately.

PERCOLATOR METHOD

STEP 2

STEP 3

STEP 4

STEP 5

SIPHON/VACUUM METHOD

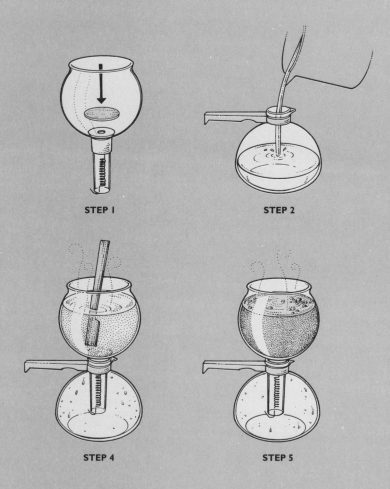

STEP 1

STEP 2

STEP 4

STEP 5

SIPHON/VACUUM

This coffee-maker uses the expansion and contraction of water vapour caused by alternating temperatures to draw hot water through coffee grounds. It requires more effort than other brewing methods but produces a clear, crisp cup.

YOU WILL NEED
Siphon/vacuum coffee-maker, digital kitchen scale, heat source, burr grinder, spoon, bamboo stirrer, coffee cups, water, freshly roasted coffee beans

METHOD
1 Set up your coffee-maker according to the manufacturer's directions. Soak the filter in warm water and then place in the correct position.

2 Depending on capacity, add 300 to 400 grams (1 ¼ to 1 ⅔ cups) of water. Put the coffee-maker over the heat source and turn it on.

3 Measure out 25 grams (about ⅓ cup) of coffee beans and use a burr grinder to grind them medium-fine.

4 When the water has transferred to the top chamber, it should be close to 95°C (203°F). Use the bamboo stirrer to make sure that the filter is in place, then add the freshly ground coffee to the upper chamber, gently agitating the water so that the grounds are fully submerged within a few seconds.

5 Reduce the heat slightly to about 90°C (194°F), but don't let it fall to a level that will cause premature dropdown. Let the coffee brew for 1 minute without stirring while it degasses and bubbles. Do not let the water boil too rapidly.

6 Remove the coffee-maker from the heat. Agitate the water with the stirrer to break the crust – the coffee will extract into the lower chamber. Remove the siphon/vacuum vessel and serve the coffee.

MACCHINETTA ESPRESSO

In Italy in particular, using a macchinetta, also known as a moka or an espresso pot, is still perhaps the most popular method of brewing coffee at home. It relies on pressurized steam to pass boiling water through the coffee grounds.

YOU WILL NEED

Kettle, macchinetta or moka or espresso pot, burr grinder, spoon, heat source, coffee cups, water, freshly roasted coffee beans

METHOD

1 Bring water to a boil in your kettle and fill the bottom chamber of the macchinetta with the boiling water up to the steam-release valve.

2 Meanwhile, finely grind your coffee beans using the burr grinder until you have enough to fill the funnel (see step 4).

3 Insert the funnel filter into the macchinetta, making sure the water does not fill the valve – empty some out, if necessary.

4 Fill the funnel with enough finely ground coffee so that it forms a rounded dome. Tap the funnel on the counter to even out the grounds.

5 Without tamping or compressing, make sure that the rubber gasket is in place and then screw the top half of the macchinetta onto the pot.

6 Place the macchinetta on the hob or other heat source, using enough heat to cover the bottom of the pot but not enough to heat the handle.

7 After 5 to 10 minutes, the macchinetta will start to gurgle. About 10 to 15 seconds after you first hear this sound, remove the pot from the heat. The coffee should continue to percolate for a while; serve as soon as it has finished percolating.

MACCHINETTA ESPRESSO METHOD

STEP 1

STEP 3

STEP 5

STEP 7

MACHINE ESPRESSO

Espresso coffee is one of the most popular coffee extraction methods, and there are numerous machines that can be used to extract an espresso shot. The quantities and timings recommended by coffee professionals differ significantly according to the type of roast, bean, style and individual taste. As a guide, the weights and measures given below are provided by coffee roasters Climpson & Sons of London, as a result of their extensive trials and tests, and are those used in their barista training classes.

ESPRESSO WEIGHTS AND MEASURES

Dose	18 to 21 grams
Extracted Weight	26 to 30 grams
Extraction Time	25 to 30 seconds

YOU WILL NEED

Espresso coffee machine with double-shot portafilter basket and grouphead, burr grinder, digital kitchen scale, spoon, tamper and mat, timer, coffee cup, water, freshly roasted coffee beans

METHOD

1 Let water run through the machine without the grouphead to flush out any old coffee grounds.

2 Grind the coffee beans to fine using the burr grinder, then remove the portafilter basket from the grouphead. Using the scale, measure out the coffee grounds into the basket, being sure that the weight is within the range specified above.

3 Level out the coffee grounds so that they are evenly distributed. As water will follow the path of least resistance, if your grounds are distributed unevenly, the water will flow through the least compacted side, leading some of the grounds to overextract and some to underextract.

MACHINE ESPRESSO METHOD

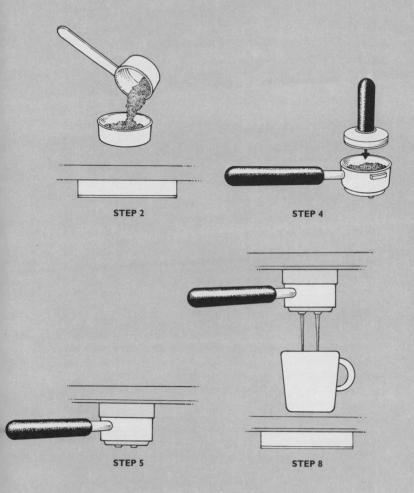

STEP 2

STEP 4

STEP 5

STEP 8

4 Click the basket back into the grouphead and then, resting the grouphead on the mat, use the tamper to press the grounds down (see panel below).

5 Put the grouphead into the espresso machine, making sure it is pulled tight.

6 Place a cup on the kitchen scale underneath the grouphead. Tare or set the scale to zero.

7 Press the button to start extraction and at the same time press start on the timer.

8 Wait for the coffee to extract, keeping an eye on the weight and time. The extracted weight should be 26 to 30 grams, extracted within 25 to 30 seconds. If the weight is over 30 grams within the 25- to 30-second time frame, you will need to grind the beans finer to slow down extraction. If the weight is less than 26 grams in the 25- to 30-second time frame, the grind needs to be coarser to speed up extraction and prevent overextraction. Serve immediately.

THE SCIENCE OF TAMPING

Many barista trainers teach how to tamp coffee using an exact amount of pressure. However, it is difficult for the home barista to measure the degree of pressure. To get as close as possible to the ideal, hold the tamper with the top in the palm of your hand. Place your thumb and index finger on opposite sides of the bottom of the tamper, then place the tamper into the portafilter basket. Using your thumb and index finger, touch the edges of both the basket and the tamper to make sure that the tamper is sitting straight. Place the grouphead on a counter low enough for you to use your body weight to press down on it. Press the coffee down, giving the tamper a swirl at the end to polish the surface. Use your hand to brush any loose grounds from the rim of the grouphead, then press down another four times, focusing on the north, south, east and west points (known as the Staub tamp) to make sure that every part of the coffee is evenly tamped. Swirl the tamper in the basket at the end to polish.

Ristretto

The ristretto shot is one of the most hotly debated types of coffee. It was originally produced using a hand-pumped espresso machine, and the handle was simply pulled twice as fast as for a traditional espresso shot. *Ristretto* translates from the Italian as 'restricted', and it produces a concentrated shot with a bolder, less bitter flavour. There are different methods of producing this type of shot; the two described here are those that are the most achievable for home baristas. The short shot method is less popular, because it excludes the soluble materials that dissolve toward the end of extraction. While these caramels and dry distillates undeniably add body and flavour, they also contribute to bitterness.

SLOWER EXTRACTION METHOD

Follow the directions for setup and extraction as detailed for machine espresso (see page 136), except either grind the beans slightly finer, which is the preferable option, or use a larger dose. This will slow down extraction, meaning that your shot will be shorter than a standard espresso (restricted) but intense and dark.

SHORT SHOT METHOD

Follow the directions for setup and extraction as detailed for machine espresso (see page 136) until the final step, where you should shorten the extraction time by 25 per cent, stopping the shot around the time blonding starts (see panel above).

MAKING ESPRESSO BEVERAGES

Americano

Legend has it that the Americano was invented for American servicemen in Europe, turning the strong European espresso into the kind of beverage they were used to at home (whether there is any truth in this story is unclear).

To prepare, extract a normal espresso shot of 30 grams (2 tablespoons) into a large mug (see page 136). Add 120 grams (½ cup) hot water to the espresso shot, then taste and continue diluting it to your desired strength.

Long Black

Popular in Australia and New Zealand, the long black is basically the reverse of an Americano, made by adding hot water to a cup and then extracting an espresso shot into the hot water (see page 136), thus retaining the crema – the top creamy layer.

MAKING ESPRESSO BEVERAGES WITH MILK

Froth your milk according to the directions on pages 52–53, creating thick, silky, hot milk ready to be poured into your coffee. Let the milk stand to settle. Prepare your espresso shot following the directions on page 136 and swirl the shot around the cup a little, mixing the crema through.

Latte

Extract an espresso shot of 30 grams (2 tablespoons) into your choice of latte glass or mug (see page 136) – these vary in capacity from 170 to 220 grams (¾ to 1 cup). Holding your glass or mug at a slight angle and the milk jug several centimetres above the rim of the receptacle, start to pour the steamed, frothed milk (see pages 52–53) at the highest point of the receptacle and, therefore, the shallowest part of the coffee; by starting at a high angle, you will be pouring some of the milk underneath the crema. Move the jug around a little, filling the cup one-third full. Lower the jug so that it is closer to the rim of the receptacle. Then, holding the jug loosely with your thumb and index finger, bring the receptacle up to your starting point and loosely wiggle the jug from side to side while moving the stream of microfoam/milk directly down the receptacle. A rosetta – a fernlike pattern – should start to form, and as you reach the bottom, quickly drag the stream up once again to finish the rosetta. It might take some practice to reach this point at the stage when your cup is full.

The ratio of coffee to milk for a latte is hotly debated, so focus on diluting the espresso to suit your individual preference, though it should generally consist of espresso and milk topped with a centimetre or so of foam.

Piccolo Latte

Simply a strong mini latte, this espresso drink is normally served in a half-size espresso glass or cup. It is prepared in the same way as a latte, but using a coffee to milk ratio of 1:1 – one part espresso to one part steamed milk, with a layer of foam on top. Different countries have different names for this beverage, such as a *café noisette* in France.

Cappuccino

You may want to select a smaller mug than for a latte – cappuccino mugs are often shallower and wider, about 180 grams (¾ cup) in capacity. Starting with the same 30-gram (2-tablespoon) espresso shot (see page 136), use the same hand movements as directed for a latte (see above). A cappuccino has less milk and more foam than a latte, so pour the milk more quickly, transferring more of the microfoam. If you are topping with unsweetened cocoa powder, stop adding milk when the mug is one-third full and add a dusting to the top of the beverage before continuing to add the remaining milk. This will create your rosetta pattern in the chocolate.

If not enough foam comes out, you can cheat; stop pouring when the cup is half full, then use a spoon to scoop extra foam on top. There is much variation to be found in the ratios between the espresso, milk and froth used according to regional practices or the particular customs of coffeehouses. The SCAA simply defines the perfect cappuccino as 'harmoniously balanced' instead of specifying exact proportions.

While cappuccino cups in countries such as the UK, USA and Australia are often large in size, the cappuccino is traditionally known as a drink of thirds in Europe. Order a cappuccino in France and you will be served a coffee that is one-third espresso, one-third milk and one-third foam dolloped on top. Ideally, the cappuccino should be stronger than the latte.

Macchiato

This is another espresso variant that is often misunderstood. It translates from the Italian as 'spotted', which is literally all you need to do with the milk. Starting with a 30-gram (2-tablespoon) espresso shot in your choice of cup (see page 136), add a dash of foamed milk to just stain the top of the espresso. Baristas in some cafés serve a macchiato in this traditional way, but others serve it 'topped up', making the drink closer to a piccolo latte (see page 141).

Cortado

Popular in Spain and Portugal, this drink is similar to a macchiato, but instead of cutting the espresso with a dash of foam, a little steamed milk is added to cut the acidity.

Flat White

Originating in Australia and New Zealand, the flat white is often served in a ceramic cup a little smaller than a cappuccino cup. Using a 30-gram (2-tablespoon) espresso shot (see page 136), pour in the velvety, blended microfoam in the same manner as you would for a latte (see page 140), but a little slower to reduce the thick foam and stopping when you are just short of the rim. The flat white is stronger than a latte, because it has a lower ratio of milk to espresso and practically no foam – just enough to cover the top, but you should be able to see milk by barely scraping the foam layer on top.

Mocha

Legend has it that this drink was named after Mocha, a seaport town in Yemen known for the exportation of coffee beans that had a distinct chocolate flavour. Other stories say that the mocha was an American invention, combining the popular hot chocolate and latte in one beverage in much the same way as other flavouring syrups, such as caramel, are added to coffee. Regardless, it is a sweet, caffeinated hot beverage that is popular worldwide. It is made in the same way as a latte (see page 140), the only difference being that 1 to 2 teaspoons of cocoa powder are added to the espresso shot and stirred in before the milk is added. It is generally served in a ceramic mug and the top dusted with unsweetened cocoa powder.

Affogato

An affogato, translating into English as 'drowned', consists of a scoop of ice cream placed in an espresso cup with a shot of espresso poured over the top, which melts the ice cream slightly – an indulgent drink often served in Italy as a dessert. The firm ice cream is eaten with a spoon, and the melted ice cream and espresso are sipped.

Corretto

Translating literally from Italian as 'corrected coffee', *caffè corretto* is another beverage that is popular in Italy as a dessert. It is simply an espresso shot with an added shot of liquor – usually sambuca, brandy or grappa (an Italian brandy).

FRENCH PRESS

This is a simple brewing method that involves steeping coffee grounds and then extracting the brewed coffee by plunging a filter down through the brew to remove the grounds from the beverage.

YOU WILL NEED
Kettle, French press, digital kitchen scale, burr grinder, spoon, timer, coffeepot (optional), coffee cups, water, freshly roasted coffee beans

METHOD

1 Fill your French press with hot water and let stand to preheat.

2 Weigh out enough coffee beans for the size of French press you are using and the strength of brew you prefer; a good starting guide is 5 to 7 grams (about 1 tablespoon) of coffee per 100 grams (scant ½ cup) of water.

3 Grind the coffee coarsely.

4 Bring fresh water to a boil and let cool for 30 seconds to 1 minute until just below boiling point.

5 Meanwhile, empty the French press of the heating water and add your coffee grounds. Place on your kitchen scale and tare or set to zero. Set the timer to 4 minutes.

6 Pour hot water over the top of the coffee in the pot to the required weight. Make sure no dry pockets of coffee remain in the bottom of the pot by giving it a stir, then start the timer.

7 Place the lid on the press but do not plunge it yet – this will help keep the heat in the pot while the coffee is brewing.

8 After 3 minutes and 45 seconds, take off the lid and use the spoon to scoop the grounds off the top. This will reduce the sediment left in the cup and prevent overextraction.

FRENCH PRESS METHOD

STEP 1

STEP 3

STEP 8

STEP 9

9 Return the lid to the pot and plunge downwards. Let settle for a few seconds, and then serve immediately. If you are not serving all the coffee immediately, pour it into another coffeepot to avoid additional extraction.

SEDIMENT

Many types of coffee leave a fine sediment in the cup after extraction. This is almost impossible to avoid, because a larger grind often results in underextraction, and tightening the filter or screen impairs flow and filters out insoluble solids or oils important for aroma and flavour.

There are a number of methods that have been devised to minimize the sediment. French press coffee-makers are designed to separate out as many of the coffee grounds as possible by having a filter that is plunged downwards through the brew to trap the grounds. However, because the filter screen has a relatively large pore size, there will still be some sediment in the coffee, although that has the benefit of retaining all the aromatic oils in the brew. The Chemex coffee-maker uses a thick paper filter that traps most of the sediment while allowing many aromatic oils to pass through. The vacuum brewing method is another low-sediment one that also permits the passage of many oils into the final beverage.

The simplest way to minimize the sediment with most brewing methods is to let the brewed coffee stand for about a minute so that all the sediment settles before pouring the coffee. Small amounts of sediment will inevitably make their way in, so simply avoid the last sip, because most of the sediment will remain at the bottom of the cup.

You may also need to check and adjust the grind size. A grind that is too fine could result in excess sediment making its way through the filtration method used. However, judging what is the appropriate level of sediment is difficult, because different methods of brewing will leave varying amounts in the cup. The best approach is to first brew your coffee on the basis of taste and cup profile, and then adjust the grind size or filtration method to reduce the sediment, instead of first trying to reduce sediment and then concentrating on achieving the flavour. Unless the coffee is left standing for a long time, sediment should not adversely affect the flavour of your brew. As such, it is one of the last things you should be concerned about in your quest for the ideal cup of coffee.

AEROPRESS

This coffee-maker uses the steeping method of brewing and a plunger and fine filter to extract the coffee. The numbers on the AeroPress correspond to the number of scoops of coffee and water you will use, each scoop making one cup – for example, for two scoops (two cups) of coffee, you need to fill your AeroPress with water until it reaches the number two. You can also use the AeroPress to measure out the water before heating it in a kettle.

YOU WILL NEED

Digital kitchen scale, burr grinder, AeroPress coffee-maker and paper micro-filter, collection vessel (cup, mug or jug), kettle, timer, water, freshly roasted coffee beans

METHOD

1 Measure your coffee beans and use the burr grinder to grind them slightly finer than for espresso. Use the scoop that comes with the AeroPress to measure the coffee – one rounded scoop should yield about 17 grams (just under 3 tablespoons) of coffee per cup of coffee.

2 Put the paper micro-filter into the AeroPress filter cap and rinse with hot water. Then rinse the AeroPress chamber with hot water to preheat it. Screw the filter onto the chamber and place the AeroPress chamber over your collection vessel.

3 Add your coffee grounds to the AeroPress chamber – there is a funnel provided with the AeroPress that you can place on top to make it easier to pour them in.

4 Measure your water and bring it to a boil in your kettle, then let stand for 30 to 60 seconds to reduce the temperature to just below boiling. The ideal water temperature is 75 to 80°C (167 to 176°F).

AEROPRESS METHOD

STEP 2

STEP 3

STEP 6

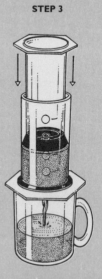

STEP 7

5 Pour a little of your measured hot water onto the coffee grounds to moisten. Use the paddle that comes with the AeroPress to give the grounds a stir for about 20 seconds.

6 Pour in the remaining hot water, reaching the number that corresponds with the number of scoops of coffee you have used.

7 Wet the black rubber ring around the plunger and place it into the top of the AeroPress. Press down slowly and watch your coffee extract into your collection vessel.

8 When the AeroPress makes a hissing sound, stop plunging and remove the coffee-maker from your collection vessel. If pressing down is too easy, your grind is probably too coarse; conversely, if pushing down is hard, your grind may be too fine. Next time, adjust your grind accordingly.

9 Dilute the coffee with hot water until it reaches your preferred strength, and serve.

COLD BREW

Cold brew coffee is often brewed overnight into a concentrate and then diluted as it is served. An advantage of cold brew is that you can refrigerate the concentrate for up to two weeks or more. Here are two ways to make it:

Toddy or Filtron Cold Brew

YOU WILL NEED

Digital kitchen scale, burr grinder, Toddy or Filtron coffee-maker, spoon, coffee cups, 1.655 kilograms (7 cups) water, 340 grams (about 4¾ cups) freshly roasted coffee beans

METHOD

1 Measure and grind the beans coarsely using the burr grinder – the grounds should have the texture of fine breadcrumbs.

2 Insert the stopper into the bottom of the brewing container. Wet the filter with cold water and place it inside the container.

3 Add 235 grams (1 cup) of water and half the grounds to the brewing container. Pour in another 710 grams (3 cups) of water slowly in a circular motion, making sure you wet all of the grounds. Add the remaining grounds and let stand for 5 minutes.

4 Slowly add the remaining 710 grams (3 cups) of water and, without stirring, lightly press down all the grounds so they are all wet. Steep for 12 to 18 hours, depending on your preferred strength.

5 When brewing is completed, remove the stopper over a container big enough to hold the coffee brew. Let the coffee filter through and then store it in the refrigerator.

6 When serving, dilute the coffee to your required strength with water or milk, beginning with a ratio of 1:1. For an iced coffee, pour some of the coffee syrup and milk over ice.

COLD BREW METHOD

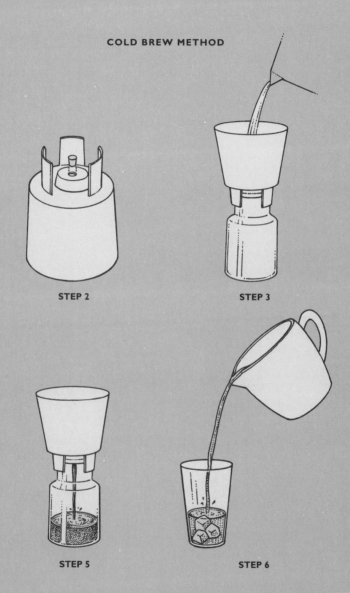

STEP 2

STEP 3

STEP 5

STEP 6

STEP 2

STEP 3

STEP 4

STEP 6

Steeped Cold Brew

YOU WILL NEED

Digital kitchen scale, burr grinder, spoon, Mason jar, saucepan with a lid or large container that can be covered, French press (see page 144) or cheesecloth and string or elastic band for covering, airtight container, coffee cups, water, freshly roasted coffee beans

METHOD

1 Measure and then grind your coffee beans coarsely using the burr grinder – the grounds should have the texture of fine breadcrumbs.

2 Add the coffee grounds to the Mason jar, saucepan or container and pour cold water over them. The ratio of grounds to water should be roughly 1:4 to 1:5, so for each cup of grounds use 4 to 5 cups of water, though you can adjust the proportions according to taste.

3 Seal or cover the jar, saucepan or container and let steep for 12 to 18 hours.

4 Once extraction is complete, you will need to filter your coffee. You can do this either by pouring it into a French press and plunging, or pouring it through a piece of cheesecloth loosely draped inside a clean container and secured around the rim of the container with string or an elastic band.

5 Store the brewed coffee concentrate in an airtight container in the refrigerator for up to two weeks.

6 To serve, dilute the coffee concentrate 1:1 with water or milk, adjusting to your preferred strength.

AFTERWORD

Coffee has made a lasting impression on our taste buds. From its discovery centuries ago right up until the present day, it has intrigued and entranced us, leading thousands of people to dedicate a huge amount of their time to searching for the perfect brew.

The invention of a plethora of machines to roast, grind, brew and serve it; the development of varied techniques and methods to extract certain flavours; or simply as a topic of conversation – coffee has pervaded many aspects of our lives. Our contemporary working and social interactions, everyday activities and recreational interludes often involve drinking a coffee of some kind, and in that way coffee offers a reflection of our social history, and the fashions and preoccupations of the day are mirrored in the brews we choose. Whether it is a cappuccino in a takeaway cup on the way to the office, a thick, syrupy espresso sipped at a café window or a single-origin pour-over expertly brewed and sipped while chatting with friends – coffee is integral to our way of life.

Bibliography

Avelino, J., Barboza, B., Araya, J. C., Fonseca, C., Davrieux, F., Guyot, B., et al. (2005). Effects of slope exposure, altitude and yield on coffee quality in two altitude terroirs of Costa Rica, Orosi, and Santa Maria de Dota. *Journal of the Science of Food and Agriculture, 85* (11), 1869–1876.

Barrett-Connor, E., Chun Chang, J., & Edelstein, S. (1994). Coffee-Associated Osteoporosis Offset by Daily Milk Consumption: The Rancho Bernardo Study. *The Journal of the American Medical Association, 271* (4), 280–283.

Calvin, C., Holzhaeuser, D., Scharf, G., Constable, A., Huber, W., & Schilter, B. (2002). Cafestol and kahweol, two coffee-specific diterpenes with anticarcinogenic activity. *Food Chem Toxicology, 40* (8), 1155–1163.

Duarte, G., & Farah, A. (2011). Effect of simultaneous consumption of milk and coffee on chlorogenic acids' bioavailability in humans. *Journal of Agricultural and Food Chemistry, 59* (14), 7925–7931.

Farah, A., Monteiro, M., & Donangelo, C. M. (2008). Biochemical, Molecular and Genetic Mechanisms: Chlorogenic Acids from Green Coffee Extract are Highly Bioavailable in Humans. *Journal of Nutrition, 138* (12), 2309–2315.

Merritt, C., Bazinet, M., Sullivan, J., & Robertson, D. (1963). Mass Spectrometric Determination of the Volatile Components from Ground Coffee. *Agricultural and Food Chemistry,* 152–155.

Noyet, S., & Nehlig, A. (2000). Dose-response study of caffeine effects on cerebral functional activity with a specific focus on dependence. *Brain Research, 858* (1), 71–77.

Queensland Government. (2013, October 23). *Coffee Processing at home.* Retrieved June 22, 2014, from Department of Agriculture, Fisheries and Forestry: http://www.daff.qld.gov.au/plants/fruit-and-vegetables/specialty-crops/coffee-processing-in-the-home

Ratnayake, W., Hollywood, R., O'Grady, E., & Stavric, B. (1993). Lipid content and composition of coffee brews prepared by different methods. *Food Chemistry Toxicology, 13* (4), 263–269.

Refiller, Bern, 2013, *Lifecycle Assessment: reusable mugs vs. disposable cups,* www.refiller.ch

Richelle, M., Tavazzi, I., & Offord, E. (2001). Comparison of the Antioxidant Activity of Commonly Consumed Polyphenolic Beverages (Coffee, Cocoa, and Tea) Prepared per Cup Serving. *J. Agric. Food Chem., 49* (7), 3438–3442.

Urgert, R., Essed, N., van der Weg, G., Kosmeijer-Schuil, T., & Katan, M. (1997). Separate effects of the coffee diterpenes cafestol and kahweol on serum lipids and liver aminotransferases. *The American Journal of Clinical Nutrition, 65* (2), 519–524.

Watanabe, T., Arai, Y., Mitsui, Y., Kusuara, T., Okawa, W., Kajihara, Y., et al. (2006). The blood pressure-lowering effect and safety of chlorogenic acid from green coffee bean extract in essential hypertension. *Clinical and experimental hypertension, 28* (5), 439–449.

Wright, G., Baker, D., Palmer, M., Stabler, D., Mustard, J., Power, E., et al. (2013). Caffeine in Floral Nectar Enhances a Pollinator's Memory of Reward. *Science, 339* (6124), 1202–1204.

Resources

Australian Specialty Coffee Association
www.aasca.com

British Coffee Association
www.britishcoffeeassociation.org

Coffee Association of Canada
www.coffeeassoc.com

Green Coffee Association
www.greencoffeeassociation.org

Institute for Scientific Information on Coffee
www.coffeeandhealth.org

International Coffee Organization
www.ico.org

National Coffee Association USA
www.ncausa.org

The Roasters Guild
www.roastersguild.org

Specialty Coffee Association of America
www.scaa.org

Speciality Coffee Association of Europe
www.scae.com

World Coffee Research
www.worldcoffeeresearch.org

Index

Acknowledgements

From Amsterdam to Melbourne I've travelled, researched and spoken to dozens of incredible people who have made coffee their life. Without these people *How to Make Coffee* would not have been possible.

Many thanks to Dan Dunne and Climpson & Sons in London for sharing their knowledge and expertise, including their espresso formula; Matthew Perger of Sensory Lab and St Ali in Melbourne for providing champion-level barista hints and tips; Counter Culture Coffee in North Carolina for providing me with their coffee flavour wheel; Roger Cook from the Institute for Scientific Information on Coffee and the Speciality Coffee Association of Europe for allowing me to share their brewing control chart with you.

A big thanks to the crew at the Deli Downstairs in Victoria Park, London; Kate, Ella and Tilly Conway; Dylan Kelly-Morgan and Rachel Kingston. All of the above supported me through those highly caffeinated months, either helping with proofreading, prompting me to consume something other than coffee or keeping me company while I tapped away at my keyboard, day after day, tucked in a corner of the Deli's refreshment room.

Of course, last but not least I would like to thank my editor, Tom Kitch; my designer, Ginny Zeal; my illustrator, Sandra Pond; my copyeditor, Jo Richardson and Ivy Press for all their hard work and support.

Image Credits